Ephesians

Probably written by a disciple of St Paul after the apostle's death, the Epistle to the Ephesians sets out God's plan to 'sum up' all things in Christ. Martin Kitchen argues that it was written partly for the good of worship generally, and partly as a reaction to the destruction of the temple at Jerusalem in 70 AD: the breaking down of the 'middle wall that divides' (Ephesians 2.14) Jew from Gentile was evidence that God had, indeed, brought the whole of human-kind together.

Ephesians understands this action of God as 'summing up' all things in Christ, which necessarily demands the co-operation of the entire Christian community. The readers are therefore urged to pursue an ethic of unity, mutually submitting to each other and growing together into a new kind of humanity.

In this innovative study, Martin Kitchen draws together historical and literary methodologies in his reading of the text, bringing his analysis into the framework of contemporary biblical criticism. This book is important reading for all theologians, students of the New Testament and ministers of religion.

Martin Kitchen is Adviser in In-Service Training in the Diocese of Southwark and a Canon Residentiary of Southwark Cathedral.

New Testament Readings
Edited by John Court
University of Kent at Canterbury

Ephesians

Martin Kitchen

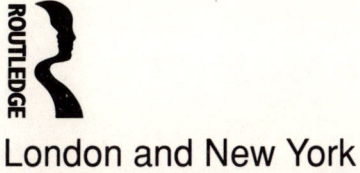

London and New York

First published 1994
by Routledge
11 New Fetter Lane, London EC4P 4EE

Simultaneously published in the USA and Canada
by Routledge
29 West 35th Street, New York, NY 10001

© 1994 Martin Kitchen

Typeset in Baskerville by
Ponting–Green Publishing Services, Chesham, Bucks
Printed and bound in Great Britain by
T.J. Press (Padstow) Ltd, Padstow, Cornwall

British Library Cataloguing in Publication Data
A catalogue record for this book is available from the
British Library.

Library of Congress Cataloging in Publication Data
Kitchen, Martin.
        Ephesians/Martin Kitchen.
            p.   cm. – (New Testament readings)
        Includes bibliographical references and index.
        1. Bible. N.T. Ephesians – Commentaries.
        I. Title.   II. Series.
    BS2695.3.K57   1994
    227'.507–dc20   94–6850

    ISBN 0–415–09506–9 (hbk)
    ISBN 0–415–09507–7 (pbk)

For Sheila

Contents

Series editor's preface

This volume has every right to stand on its own, as a significant contribution to the study of the book of the New Testament with which it is concerned. But equally it is a volume in a series entitled *New Testament Readings*. Each volume in this series deals with an individual book among the early Christian writings within, or close to the borders of, the New Testament. The series is not another set of traditional commentaries, but designed as a group of individual interpretations or 'readings' of the texts, offering fresh and stimulating methods of approach. While the contributors may be provocative in their choice of a certain perspective, they also seek to do justice to a range of modern methods and provide a context for the study of this particular text.

The collective object of the series is to share with the widest readership the extensive range of recent approaches to Scripture. There is no doubt that literary methods have presented what amounts to a 'new look' to the Bible in recent years. But we should not neglect to ask some historical questions or apply suitable methods of criticism from the Social Sciences. The origins of this series are in a practical research programme at the University of Kent, with an exclusive concern about ways of using the Bible. It is to be hoped that our series will offer fresh insights to all who, for any reason, study or use these books of the early Christians.

John M. Court
Series Editor

Preface

So many have contributed in various ways to this book that it seems invidious to claim credit for it as my own. My parents taught me to pray and, with the help of the Salvation Army, first introduced me to the possibilities of Christian soldiery. The Reverend Kenneth Paterson, late Minister of Trinity Road Chapel, Upper Tooting, London, began preaching in 1968 a series of sermons on the Epistle to the Ephesians which stimulated my thinking on its theological themes.

Doctor, later Professor, Graham Stanton, of King's College, London, a fellow former euphonium player, and a constant friend through many changes, gently introduced me to the complexities and wonders of New Testament criticism. Professor Christopher Evans showed me – along with how many others? – how to combine a rigorously inquisitive approach to the text of the New Testament with a serious, though never solemn, commitment to Christian discipleship. He supervised my earliest attempts at New Testament research and introduced me to Christian literature which I should never otherwise have read. He gave generously of his time, his knowledge and his spirit in ways that defy either thanks or re-compense. Canon, later Professor, Leslie Houlden, took on a still somewhat gauche research student and encouraged me to read widely in the area of literary criticism. Professor Barnabas Lindars, whose untimely death still saddens me, provided an inimitably kind combination of persuasion, compassion and encouragement, until the research was duly completed and the thesis presented upon which this book is based.

Colleagues at Manchester Polytechnic (now the Manchester Metropolitan University) and at the Chaplaincy to Higher Education in Manchester – especially John Price, David Melling,

Kenneth Stevenson and Alan Tiltman – provided constant stimulation and support. Bishop Ronnie Bowlby generously allowed me to begin my present job by completing the write-up of my research. With characteristic cheerfulness his successor, Bishop Roy Williamson, has encouraged the writing of this book, as well as so many other aspects of my work. Professor Peter Selby, when Bishop of Kingston, provided the opportunity for some of its themes to be discussed with groups of clergy in the Kingston Episcopal Area, and other colleagues – clergy and lay ministers in the Diocese of Southwark (some of them might be surprised) – have provided varied and valuable intellectual stimulus.

Dr John Court, the editor of this series of *Readings*, has made many helpful suggestions, and Richard Stoneman and Diana Grivas of Routledge have shown remarkable patience.

The love, care and nourishment provided by my wife, Sheila, exceed the praises sung in the last chapter of the book of Proverbs and in the sustained lyricism of the Song of Songs. I can never repay her what I owe, but nevertheless dedicate this book to her.

Note on the text

Throughout the book the English translation of New Testament passages, including the Epistle to the Ephesians, is usually that of the writer direct from the Greek.

References to the text of Ephesians are normally without the preceding title (e.g. 1.1). Where other biblical books are quoted or referred to, the name is given with the reference (e.g. Colossians 1.1).

Chapter 1

An introduction to a reading of Ephesians

'The Epistle of St Paul the Apostle to the Ephesians' arouses a variety of responses in its readers. It was described by Coleridge (1835) as 'the divinest composition of man', and by one commentator as 'the quintessence of Paulinism' (Peake 1917: 285). However, the majority of scholarly opinion now casts doubt upon its supposed Pauline authorship; it is a notorious fact of early church history that many of Paul's contemporaries doubted his claim to apostleship; there are those who question whether Ephesians can properly be called an 'epistle' at all; and the earliest texts lack the words 'in Ephesus' in Ephesians 1.1.

These responses indicate both the historical and the literary questions which confront any reader of this sometimes baffling document, and of which the reader needs to be aware before coming to the text itself. The purpose of this chapter will therefore be to discuss Ephesians as history and as literature, by way of an introduction to a reading of the epistle.

EPHESIANS AS HISTORY

The assumption that scholars hitherto have made is that, in order to read the Bible properly, it is essential to understand how it had been read in the past, and, in particular, how its author intended it to be understood. This is not altogether surprising; Christianity has long maintained that it is an 'historical' religion, in that it has taught that God, 'beyond history', has intervened and made a difference to it. A certain set of assumptions and beliefs at the philosophical level made that view possible, and, indeed, inevitable. However, this set of philosophical assumptions is subject to questioning today, so much so that Christianity is now being called to understand itself in rather different terms.

Why is this so? There is not much room here to discuss this in detail, but an outline of the shift in consciousness may be briefly traced. There are still those who take the view that the New Testament scholar is primarily an historian, because the New Testament itself is primarily an historical document. For Marshall (1977) this is due to a conviction that the events narrated, in the gospels in particular, are the basis of the faith of believers today. Kaufmann also states the primacy of historical study of the Bible:

> We are not concerned to recover simply 'What the Bible says'; we are seeking to find out 'What actually happened' in Israel and the early Christian Church, so that we will be in a position to assess the claim that God himself was active there, making himself known to all mankind through that particular historical development.
>
> (1971: 140)

The historian Leopold von Ranke (1874) first highlighted the aim to write history '*wie es eigentlich gewesen ist*' – 'as it really happened' – and Strauss's *Life of Jesus, Critically Examined* (1846) applied this principle to the story of Jesus. So began the process of erosion of the 'historical' foundations of Christian belief. His influence continued into this century, with Bultmann becoming, perhaps, the most famous for historical scepticism. Bultmann's claim to fame rests also on his joining such scepticism with an existentialist hermeneutic, which concentrated on 'the meaning of the text for today'. Historical scepticism is even further advanced now, and the very proliferation of recent attempts (Edwards 1992; Wilson 1992; Wright 1992; Thiering 1993) to start yet another 'quest of the historical Jesus', such as was undertaken in the nineteenth century and brilliantly documented by Schweitzer (1910), is an indication of the near impossibility of this approach, and illustrates the truth of Schama's confession, concerning historians generally, 'We are doomed to be forever hailing someone who has just gone around the corner and out of earshot' (1991: 320).

In part, the problem with the exclusively historical approach is that the text has been exploded by the success of the method, and a greater hermeneutical problem has thereby been created. The critical study of history began at more or less the same time as the critical study of the Bible, and as the dogmatic assertions of theologians concerning the nature of the Bible came to be subjected, one by one, to critical enquiry, the edifice of biblical theology, in so far as it was conceived as a unified structure, was gradually dismantled. The gospels were discovered to have been written by authors who were neither apostles nor eye-witnesses; as theology was seen to determine narrative, so the teachings of the apostle Paul were inevitably relativized. Indeed, the whole study of history developed away from the attempt to trace overall movement or design and became instead the minute amassment of the smallest of data, in the attempt to recover, in the case of any incident, *wie es eigentlich gewesen ist.*

Nineham (1978) represents perhaps the most acute understanding amongst theologians of this state of affairs when he observes that historical events are 'encapsulated in their own time and are thus essentially irrecoverable by any future generation'. Nineham's starting point is the inevitability of cultural change and cultural pluralism. As societies, and the people who comprise them, undergo change, so also do the 'doctrines felt as facts' (to use Hulme's expression), or the 'constellation(s) of absolute presuppositions' (to use that of Collingwood). The Bible suffers in the same way, for it, too, emanates from a world vastly different from that of our day, and yet there is the added temptation for Christians to believe that ways of relating to it may continue unquestioned. Nineham rejects the 'solutions' both of claiming that the text 'really' means something different from what it purports to say, and of asserting that the revelation of God was in the historical events recorded in the Bible, but not in the biblical record of them.

Neither does Nineham consider satisfactory the approach of 'biblical theology' to this problem, because it created a special class of 'historical' event, of the validity of which Nineham is by no means certain; it seemed to require special pleading on behalf of biblical events, in order to assign them greater historical probability. The events related in the Bible cannot be excluded from the general characteristics of all historical events. Nineham sees the 'nub of the matter' as the early Christians' experience of a new relationship with God, which is not so much 'documented', but rather 'legitimated', by the biblical records.

Some would consider Nineham as unduly conservative. Can 'encapsulated' events of history be said to exist? If they are not accessible, are they not as good as non-existent? The 'problem of history' now confronts the reader of any text in a particularly acute form. For the text emerges from history, it has a history, and it constructs history. It might be tempting to say therefore that the text *conveys* history, but it very soon becomes clear, rather, that the text simply conveys itself; whatever texts say, they say on their own authority. 'There is nothing outside the text,' we are now told.

Alongside the rise of historical study, there grew the suspicion of supernaturalism which was begun by the work of Reimarus. His *Fragments of an Unknown Author* were published by the writer and critic, Gotthold Ephraim Lessing, in Wolfenbüttel between 1774 and 1778. His influence continues through the Enlightenment to the present day. However, the fact that faith has not altogether been eroded by historical criticism is an indication, not of irrationalism in the persistence of religion, but of the fact that the primary concern of religious people is not what happened in the past, but what may sustain, nourish or challenge their faith. In other words, people go to church to worship, not to learn history; their business is with God as with a living concern. The recital of events – and their re-enactment in liturgy – is something other than a history lesson.

The question of authorship

The question of history as it affects the Epistle to the Ephesians is closely bound up with that of authorship. Ephesians was known to the 'Apostolic Fathers' – Ignatius of Antioch, Polycarp of Smyrna and Hermas – who lived and wrote a generation after most of the New Testament documents themselves were produced (Lake 1976). Later it was the subject of homiletical treatment by Jerome (PL 26: 439–554), John Chrysostom (PG 62: 9 176) and Theodore of Mopsuestia (Swete 1880: 253). As is common in the patristic period, the Fathers' approach to the epistle reflects the preaching and teaching needs of the church of their respective days and circumstances, and their treatment of it is largely concerned with the refutation of error in the church (as the writers saw it), and with the edification of Christian congregations. They tend to regard the epistle as teaching the true doctrine of the church, and so undergirding their own theological position. The assumption that Paul wrote it was not questioned until modern times (except that Theodore of Mopsuestia expressed surprise at the epistle's omission of any sign that the author had personal knowledge of the church at Ephesus, although Paul is said in Acts 19 to have spent some time there).

Modern, critical study of the Epistle to the Ephesians may be said to have begun with Erasmus of Rotterdam (1519), who first observed, 'It can be regarded as [the work] of another.' The English Unitarian scholar Evanson (1792) subsequently argued that the differences between the address of the epistle and its contents pointed to authorship by someone other than Paul. The case against Pauline authorship of Ephesians was first set out in detail by de Wette (1847), and his arguments have dominated the discussion ever since:

1 the literary dependence of Ephesians upon Colossians;
2 the distinctive style of the epistle, and in particular the use of relative clauses, participles, prepositional phrases and genitival constructions;
3 the presence of certain expressions which indicate a post-apostolic date, such as 'on the foundation of the apostles and prophets' (2.20) and 'the holy apostles and prophets' (3.5).

Subsequent scholarship saw opinion upon the authenticity of Ephesians divided, but the tendency was in favour of pseudonymity. Baur (1845) and Schwegler (1846), of the University of Tübingen, denied Ephesians to Paul, and saw it as the result of the process, worked out in the early history of the church, of a Hegelian dialectic between 'Petrine' and 'Pauline' Christianity, traceable respectively to the apostles Peter and Paul. This dialectic reached its synthesis in 'primitive catholicism', which developed in the later second century, and Ephesians is to be dated around this time. (Such application of the philosophy of Hegel to the early history of the church became the hallmark of the so-called 'Tübingen School' of New Testament interpretation.) Holtzmann (1872) was of the same opinion and argued that the redactor of Ephesians made use of an earlier version of Colossians when writing Ephesians. Abbott (1897), on the other hand, took very seriously the patristic testimony to Ephesians, rejected the arguments from the language and the 'line of thought' of the epistle, and was persuaded that its personal references could only be from the pen of the apostle himself. Jülicher (1904) and Cadbury (1959) found it almost impossible to make up their minds, and Robinson's commentary (1904), for a long time the major commentary on the epistle in the English language, did not even raise the question. Goodspeed

(1933, 1956) and Knox (1942, 1959) developed a significant theory about the epistle's origin, and a number of other scholars writing in the 1950s and 1960s – including Maurer (1951), Dibelius (1953), Nineham (1956), Käsemann (1958), Bornkamm (1948) and Conzelmann (1962) – also found strong reasons for denying Ephesians to Paul himself.

The most comprehensive discussion of the arguments against Pauline authorship in recent years remains the work of Mitton (1951), which he endorsed in his subsequent commentary (1976). He states first the linguistic arguments, noting the number of words and phrases in Ephesians which are not found elsewhere in the Pauline corpus. For example, where Ephesians has the word 'devil' (4.27; 6.11), Paul would be more likely to use the word 'Satan', and phrases such as 'in the heavenlies' (1.3,20; 2.6; 3.10; 6.12), 'the father of glory' (1.17), 'before the foundation of the world' (1.4) and 'be knowing' (5.5) are also untypical of Paul himself. Mitton also refers to the epistle's 'unparalleled number of genitival formulations', such as 'praise of his glory' (1.6,12,14), 'joint of provision' (4.16) and 'desires of deceitfulness' (4.22), as uncharacteristic of Paul's style.

Second, Mitton deals with stylistic arguments, repeating the observation of Sanday and Headlam (1914) that Paul's own style is 'rapid, terse and incisive', whereas the sentences of Ephesians are long and ponderous, their average length being 1.4 lines in Romans, and 3.0 in Ephesians.

Third, Mitton speaks of literary arguments, and in particular the dependence of Ephesians upon Colossians. One third of the content of Colossians is to be found in Ephesians, he notes, and what is more, words such as 'mystery' (1.9; 3.3; 5.32; 6.19), 'economy' (1.10; 3.2,9) and 'fulness' (1.10,23; 3.19) are used in different senses. Such personal references as there are seem artificial, unlike the genuine letters of Paul.

Fourth, turning to historical arguments, Mitton notes that the community's life indicates a set of circumstances later than those appertaining in the time of Paul. In particular, the question of the place of the Gentiles within the church, which had constituted a major – if not the major – theological problem for Paul, is replaced in Ephesians with the problem of how a largely Gentile church is to regard and treat the Jews.

Finally, there are what Mitton calls 'doctrinal' arguments:

1 the fact that the universal church (1.22; 3.10,21; 5.23,24,27) has replaced the local congregation as the object of theological reflection, that it is regarded as the 'bride' of Christ, and that the question of circumcision is now resolved, to be replaced by the problem of the church's unity;

2 the fact that 'apostles and prophets' (3.5) are now regarded as the foundation of the church, whereas for Paul (in 1 Corinthians 3.11) this foundation could be none other than Christ himself. These same apostles and prophets are referred to as 'holy', and it is unlikely that Paul would have regarded himself thus;

3 the fact that the parousia is now no longer regarded as an imminent event; rather, a long future in history is envisaged for the church in 2.7; 4.13; 3.21. This affects what is said about marriage: in 1 Corinthians Paul had discouraged it, whereas here it is given special honour as the image of Christ's relationship with the church. The delay of the parousia also has implications for the upbringing of children – they are to be brought up 'in the discipline and instruction of the Lord'.

The reader is faced with two options. Either Paul allowed his style, language and thought to develop to such an extent in all these respects, or another writer so breathed the atmosphere of Paul's thought, perceived in Paul's writing the essence of the gospel as he understood it, and used his knowledge of Pauline tradition to inspire an 'epistle' of his own in conscious continuity with the voice of an apostle, with its own particular language, style and theological emphases. The latter position has increasingly been that adopted by scholars, and this is the view adopted in this *Reading*; Ephesians is a pseudepigraph by a Pauline disciple.

The question of purpose

With the growing consensus that Ephesians was not written by Paul himself, scholars turned to the question, In what circumstances was the epistle written, and for what purpose?

We have already noted the view of Baur and Schwegler, of the 'Tübingen School'. Goodspeed (1933, 1956) and Knox (1942, 1959) thought that the original collector of the Pauline corpus of letters was inspired to that task by his reading of two documents, St Luke's Gospel and the Acts of the Apostles (known together as Luke–Acts and most probably written by the same person). This collector sent for copies of Paul's letters to the churches mentioned in Acts, immersed himself in their theology and ethics, and then proceeded to write an introduction to the collected corpus. This collector was the same Onesimus referred to in Paul's letter to Philemon, who, according to Goodspeed, subsequently became bishop of Ephesus. Mitton (1951) also adopted a version of this theory.

Chadwick (1960), though uncertain of the epistle's authorship, thought that Ephesians was written in response to a crisis of faith among Gentile Christians. They were beginning to doubt their position in the divine plan for the world, since their coming to faith was so late in time. The prevailing view in the ancient world was that age guaranteed truth and validity; the epistle assured them of their status in the divine economy by pointing out their continuity with Judaism, which dated back before Moses to Abraham. The claims of Paul's gospel of Jesus Christ were therefore rooted in God's ancient plans for Israel.

Kirby (1968) drew attention to those aspects of Ephesians which seem to suggest the context of baptism, and came to the conclusion that the epistle arose out of the baptismal liturgy of the early church. He showed how it has links with synagogue worship and with Jewish traditions concerning the feast of Pentecost. Following upon the work of Dahl (1951), he developed the theory that, as Pentecost marked the renewal of the covenant for Israel, so, in Christian tradition, it took on associations of baptism. These came together in Ephesians in a liturgical text celebrating these various elements, along with those of the giving of the Law in Judaism and the coming of the Spirit to the church.

Fischer's (1973) attempt to explain the setting and the purpose of Ephesians dates its writing to a 'transitional period between apostolic and post-apostolic times'. In this period the church was becoming more institutionalized, at the expense of 'charismatic' leadership, when growth in power of the bishops resulted in the suppression of mission. At the same time, according to Fischer, the Gentile majority in the church was wanting to reject its Jewish heritage. Fischer saw the author of Ephesians as a Pauline disciple who recognized these dangers and wrote under the name of Paul because he lacked any authority for himself. He attempted to uphold a concept of mission rather than to impose a formal order of church leadership – and this sets him apart from other writers of both that and the immediately succeeding period. His references, for example, to apostles and prophets (3.5), rather than to bishops, presbyters and deacons, as in the epistles to Timothy and Titus and the Apostolic Fathers, were an attempt to re-establish the earlier, purer, Spirit-led order of church government.

For Fischer, the writer of Ephesians was making a final attempt to salvage the church's unity, for the rejection of its Jewish heritage would be to the detriment of the Gentiles themselves. He intended to conciliate rather than to polemicize, hence the 'longwindedness' of his style, which is the sign of a search for a compromise. However, the attempt to reconcile the Jewish and Gentile wings of the church ended in failure; the church did lose its missionary thrust, and 'primitive catholicism' did win the day. Fischer's is a brilliant thesis, worked out with great skill and learning. However, it contains several weaknesses: episcopacy was not the enemy of charisma, and there is no evidence that the church lost its missionary thrust towards the end of the first century. The nature of pseudepigraphy is complex, and the desire to write with authority constitutes but one strand in its employment, as we shall see later. The references to apostles and prophets are not part of some antipathy towards bishops, presbyters and deacons, but reflect a different time and different concerns. Finally, 'mission' is not the driving theme behind the theology of Ephesians.

A monograph by Meyer (1977) a few years after Fischer's work also focused upon the missionary task of the church, arguing that the writer of the epistle set out to integrate the missionary concern of the Pauline tradition with a conception of the church's witness to the divine will of universal salvation in Christ, of which the reconciliation of Jew and Gentile is a foretaste.

However, this emphasis on mission is not supported by the text. There is little in the epistle that urges either the sharing of faith or service to the world, and an examination of the word 'gospel' yields the conclusion that it is used purely in order to indicate what has been achieved in the church. The only exception to this is in 6.19, where it is simply part of the 'Pauline' framework, designed to portray Paul's concern for preaching the gospel. The writer makes no mention of any expectation that his readers will continue the task. The same is true for the content of Ephesians 3, where Paul is portrayed as the 'apostle to the Gentiles'; the effect of this is not to encourage mission, but to magnify the significance of Paul in the minds of his readers.

There is therefore no consensus about the purpose for which Ephesians was written. The collection and publication of the 'canon' of Paul's letters; the doctrine of baptism; the historical phenomenon of 'primitive catholicism'; the demands of mission – all prove of no help in ascertaining why this text might have been written. Other approaches to the text are needed.

EPHESIANS AS LITERATURE

Morgan and Barton (1988) highlight the impasse which historical studies of the Bible have reached and which this brief survey has traced. They suggest that a more fruitful approach is to take seriously the insights of literary criticism, which may prove more amenable to the religious concerns of the community for which the Bible is a sacred text. A way into this discussion is provided with the observation that Ephesians is an 'epistle', a letter. Indeed, the epistles are the earliest documents in the New Testament.

Wilder (1964) maintained that the writers of the New Testament were reluctant to commit pen to paper. His survey of the literary genres of the New Testament shows how the events surrounding the life, ministry, death and resurrection of Jesus had a profound effect upon the *language* of the earliest communities, and this was marked, in particular, by its immediacy and 'orality'. This, in turn, was clearly connected with assumptions about the imminence of the end, and the early Christians turned to writing as this hope dwindled. Paul himself clearly regarded his letters as written – just as his apostleship was exercised – 'on borrowed time'. The letter to the Ephesians, however, is mannered in its literary characteristics. Here is no writer reluctant to pick up his pen; rather, here is someone conscious of his literary heritage in Paul the apostle who, whether reluctantly or otherwise, began this tradition of 'epistolary' writing within the church. Since the writer of Ephesians positively delights in the possibilities of written language, as Wilder observes, his own claim concerning the church's reluctance to write is seen to be inadequate. By the time of the writing of the earliest pseudepigraphs, such as Ephesians, and of the gospels, Christianity had become, like Judaism, a *writing* religion. Bailey and Vander Broek (1992: 27–30) explore the implications of the study of genre for the exegesis of the text.

Life-setting

The term 'setting in life' (German, *Sitz im Leben*) was coined to refer to the context within the early Christian communities in which sayings, statements and parables of Jesus might have arisen and been attributed to him prior to and in the process of the writing of the four Gospels. One important 'setting' was the worship of those communities. With the exception of Dahl (1951) and Kirby (1968), commentators have not taken particularly seriously the fact that the life-setting of the New Testament letters, and especially of Ephesians, was the worship of the Christian community. This context of worship is evident from such passages as 1 Thessalonians 5.27, 'I adjure you by the Lord to have this letter read to them all', and Colossians 4.16, 'Once this letter has been read among you, see that it is read also to the church at Laodicea, and that you in turn read my letter to Laodicea.' As Best observes (1972), such commands express Paul's concern that his letters be read aloud to the gathered community, so that none of those present should fail to hear what is said.

The public reading of scripture was inherited from the practice of Jewish synagogues, and there are examples of this in Luke (4.16–27) and Acts (13.15,27; 15.21). The reading of the writings of apostles in the Christian communities was added very early to the reading of the law and the prophets, with greater prominence being accorded to the writings after their writer's death. These writings came to be venerated, in due course of time, as 'Holy Scripture'. The New Testament was written to aid worship, and so became an integral part of it. Ephesians is, therefore, not simply an historical document, but also part of a canon of scripture in a religious tradition. This is not to say that the religious tradition, in the form of systematic statements of doctrine, can alone determine the interpretation of the text – even though it did before the rise of historical–critical scholarship. On the contrary, exegetical and hermeneutical questions need to interact with what may be discovered by critical enquiry concerning the text of scripture, so that the church's continuing reflection on its contemporary life may be seen to be in conversation with its scriptural and traditional heritage. Scriptures gain their significance principally through the part they play in the life of the Christian community, which is constituted and which meets together primarily for worship. The concrete realities of the community's life, therefore, cannot but be an element in the understanding of the text.

In the case of Ephesians, the omission of the liturgical dimension from the last few centuries' research is all the more striking, since the epistle itself breathes the language of worship and prayer. Theologians have recently been exploring the relationship between liturgy and theology. Ramsey (1936) put forward the view that the one, great, unifying feature of the church's many and various divisions was its universal recital of the Lord's Prayer. He put forward the view that Christian praying is essentially linked with the church's liturgy. It is this, especially the rite of the Eucharist, which brings into focus the oneness of the church. Christian 'truth' is the expression of this worship, which is rooted in the gospel and which, in turn, is centred upon the passion of Christ.

More recently, Wainwright (1980) has re-asserted the ancient precept that the church's theological enterprise arises from its worship, and not the other way round, as in the well-known Latin tag, *lex orandi, lex credendi* ('what people pray is what they believe'). Wainwright constructs a systematic theology upon the basis of the liturgy of the gathered community, observing that the Bible as an actual book serves as 'some kind of sacrament of the Word of God' (1980: 149). Liturgy is behind scripture, and this has implications for the use of scripture in the church. He notes that it is now generally agreed that the Old and New Testaments contain much material which originated in the context of worship. Liturgy functions as a hermeneutical continuum in that the liturgy has contributed to the preservation and transmission of the text; liturgy is therefore the pre-eminent setting in which the church ponders and applies the scriptures. He notes that scholars such as Barr (1973) and Evans (1975) have recognized the contribution which liturgy may have to make towards surmounting the historico-cultural gulf between the ancient writings and the present community – even though both see this as only a partial solution, requiring interpretive work in theology and preaching.

One danger of this view might be to suggest that the Bible should *only* be read in church and that theology is not a proper discipline for study in 'secular' contexts. While this would be an extreme view, Wainwright has nevertheless made plain the roots of the biblical material in the worship of the Christian community, and his basic thesis cannot be denied; it was the church's worship which gave rise to its scriptures. It is therefore appropriate that consideration should be given to that context of worship as the scriptures are expounded.

Kavanagh (1984) is another theologian to insist upon an understanding of the Bible and of theology that recognizes the liturgical origins of both. He takes as his starting point the precise words of Prosper of Aquitaine from which the Latin tag is derived, *lex supplicandi legem statuat credendi* (roughly, 'the substance of prayer is the foundation for the substance of belief'), acknowledges the radical implications of this assertion and develops a liturgical theology upon this basis. His starting point is the world, and in particular the city, which he regards as a microcosm of the world. The human race, he claims, 'has always regarded its cities as dynamic and holy icons of the World'. His acute analysis of this contemporary world is marked by a passionate concern and an almost prophetic despair. He traces the decline of urban life from Rousseau to the present day, noticing how the image of the 'noble savage' has influenced our civilization, to a point at which 'the city's sacred potentialities have been removed and invested in the sovereign individual' (1984: 26).

The redemption of the city is the discovery of the human position within it, and the removal of 'world alienation'. Turning to the Bible, he remarks that if the Book of Genesis, at the beginning of the Bible, represents Alpha and the Book of Revelation, at the end, represents Omega, then the letter to the Hebrews 'is the hinge that joins the other two together'. By this he means that between the 'Fall' in Genesis 3 and the 'Banquet of the Lamb' in Revelation 19 there must take place the resolution of the conflicts of human society in which the shedding of blood is an action performed not 'for the sheer hell of it' – and the letter to the Hebrews has much to say about priesthood and sacrifice. Kavanagh understands the sacrifice of Christ, and its memorial in the Eucharist, within this context, of 'slaying rightly', and he appeals to the Epistle to the Hebrews for the image of 'a perfect Lamb who leads all of us to the World's altar and then concelebrates there his own sacrifice with all that is' (1984: 35).

The liturgy of the church is thus placed very firmly in the context of the world, and it effects the sacralizing of the human city. 'When we walk in our city, therefore, we walk always on holy ground' (1984: 38). What Kavanagh regards as the urban emphasis of the Judaeo-Christian tradition is thus not the mark of a religion which is set against nature and the world. It is rather that these are not regarded as 'the Problem'. The problem with the world is humanity which inhabits it, and which organizes its life principally within its cities. Kavanagh thus places liturgical language and, specifically, sacramental language – that is, primarily, language which speaks of the Christian Eucharist – at the head of the church's theological agenda, even though he recognizes that this is the other way round from that in which most Christian people are accustomed to think. He regretfully concludes that the result of this reversal has been the 'enthusiastic trivializing' of the gospel; 'artifact has become plaything, *sacramentum* a rubber duck' (1984: 47). What has been lost is the sense of 'imaging' which is necessary for knowledge; 'discourse thickens meaning found in reality and then increments that meaning with style.' Sacramental discourse is of this order.

Far from leaving the church preoccupied solely with its own concerns, therefore, he recalls its life and worship in the age of the Fathers, when the liturgy would last for most of the day, and embrace the whole of the city (1984: 57–60). Kavanagh points out that its concerns are fundamentally those of the world, because it is to the renewal of the world that Christ was – and consequently his body, the church is – committed. Similarly, the concern of Ephesians is for the whole world. Its theology begins in the context of worship, and its theological understanding is both cosmic in its extent and material in its emphasis. Like the letter to the Hebrews in Kavanagh's scheme, Ephesians finds a point of unity in the sacrifice of Christ, who incorporated both Jew and Gentile in his one body (2.11–22). In celebrating the mystery of God in Christ, Ephesians tells a story about God's interaction with the world. This story, as it is recited in the church, has moral consequences for the human community.

The rhetoric of Ephesians

Literary theory since Gadamer (1975) has made us wary of any attempt to discover the intentions of the authors of texts. Texts, however, have a purpose, and that purpose is persuasion, and this is the function of rhetoric (Eagleton 1983). Persuasion may be of the truth of a set of propositions, or it may be towards a certain kind of action; most New Testament texts attempt both of these. It may be argued that Ephesians simply builds upon the hellenistic tradition of epistolary writing: it attempts to persuade its readers of the validity of its argument and the correctness of its ethic. Recent work on the nature of Christian theology has concentrated on the concept of 'story', and has developed the concept of 'narrative theology'. This category sheds some light upon the literary problems of the New Testament and theological writing in general. The appeal of narrative theology can hardly be regarded as surprising, since there is so much narrative to be taken into account, both in the Bible and in subsequent Christian theology. The texts of the gospels, the way salvation history is understood in the epistles, and the way that Christian theologians have come to speak of God's dealings with the world in incarnation, crucifixion and resurrection all have a distinctly narrative character.

Stroup's survey and discussion of this approach (1981) roots the emergence of narrative theology in a two-fold crisis in the modern world. On the one hand, there is a crisis of Christian identity, which is related to the individual experience of many, who are aware of a crisis of personal identity in the modern world. On the other hand there is a crisis in the religious concept of revelation. Stroup maintains that narrative is an essential part of personal identity; that is, the psychological integrity of a human being is closely allied to the extent to which men and women are aware of and able to recount their life story.

Taking account of the current doubts among scholars concerning the hegemony of the historical critical method, Stroup asserts the primacy of the text 'in the life of the community', though he affirms the centrality of historical study of the text. However, 'the most intriguing question is why narrative is such a primary genre in scripture', he says, and that for two reasons. The first is that 'the identity of a community ... requires the interpretation of historical experience, and the narrative seems to be the appropriate literary genre for articulating and interpreting the past.' The other reason is theological, that the faith of Jews and Christians is radically this-worldly and historical. Redemption and salvation are not just images or ideas, but realities which are understood to be rooted in events that happened in the past, and realities which continue to unfold in the present and the future (1981: 145–6).

Stroup's approach to the text is based on the 'historical' rather than the 'textual', but the emphasis on the function of narrative for the identity of the person and for the nature of theology is important. The question does arise, of course, of how 'story' is related to the genre of 'epistle'. Letters are occasional writings, and they do not undergo repetition and recension to the same degree as do various kinds of narrative; their life is short and their influence ephemeral. Nevertheless, in the context of theology, they relate closely to the Christian story, as it is re-enacted in the worship of the community which gave and gives birth to it. Sometimes letters carry the story, sometimes they imply it, sometimes they comment upon it. A narrative is implied in Ephesians, and an ethic is both implied in the narrative and extrapolated from it.

By nature provisional, the letter, both in form and in content, performs a number of functions. First, it recalls to the mind of the community the presence and absence of the person who wrote it, whether or not he or she is still alive, and whether or not the letter is authentic. Second, it focuses the attention of the community on the Christian story, and applies it to its life. Third, it reminds the community that the story is still to be heard and reflected upon, within the context of the worship of God.

How, then, does the text of Ephesians set out to achieve its purpose? For the student of rhetoric, the *structure* of any writing is significant. Doty (1973) identified the structure of ancient letters as: (a) introduction, (b) text or body, and (c) conclusion. White's analysis (1972) of the 'body' of the Greek letter compared it with that of Paul's letters. He observed the more closely-knit structure of the letters of Paul, in which the writer both developed more carefully the argument or theme, and incorporated the literary conventions into his theological argument. He also noted the subtle change given by Paul to the end of the body of the letter, in which Paul brings together an expression of his confidence in the addressees (that they will comply with his desires), and the assertion of his own expected appearance or 'parousia' among them.

Funk (1966: 267) observed that one particular feature of the Pauline letters was the 'travelogue', which is present also in other New Testament documents. He observed that the ending of 1 Corinthians focuses not on the *eschaton* (the final event of history, or the coming of the Lord), but on the apostle's proposed visit; the travelogue is also to be found in the body of the letter in Philippians and 1 Thessalonians. The Epistle to the Galatians has no travelogue, but Galatians 4.12–20 provides a 'surrogate'; a visit by the apostle is impossible, so he contents himself with the recollection of his former visit. The travelogue is related to the body of the letter in the same way that the promise (or threat) of an oral word is related to the written word in Paul's disposition toward language. Funk's observations lead him to posit 'the following working hypothesis' concerning the substructure of the Pauline letter form:

1 salutation;
2 thanksgiving;
3 body, with formal opening, connective and transitional formulae, concluding eschatological climax and travelogue;
4 paraenesis;
5 closing elements.

Ephesians corresponds to some degree with the structure delineated by Funk, even though there is sufficient variation to show that the letter is the work of a Pauline disciple, rather than of the apostle himself. The extent of the agreement indicates the extent to which the structure was imitated by Paul's successors. It may be set out as follows:

1 salutation;
2 blessing and thanksgiving;
3 body, without formal opening, but with connective and transitional formulae which render it possible to be regarded as an extension of the thanksgiving; the 'travelogue' is the reference in Ephesians 3 to Paul's extensive travels for the sake of the gospel as 'apostle to the Gentiles';
4 paraenesis;
5 closing elements.

It will become clear, as we continue our *Reading* of Ephesians, that its structure is designed to convey its argument, for after the 'blessing', the 'thanksgiving' shades into the body of the letter, which also comprises the 'memorial' to Paul and the celebration of his legacy to the church. The paraenesis in chapters four to six comprises five sections of ethical material. This develops with the use (in 4.1,17; 5.2,8,15) of the verb *peripatein* ('to walk'), a well-known rhetorical device in Rabbinic writing, which, significantly, indicates the epistle's debt to Jewish as much as to hellenistic literary convention.

The work of recent scholars has attempted to relocate the study of the New Testament documents within the boundaries of general literary criticism, as it is understood by students of literature. This has meant 'trying to understand the biblical books by methods of approach and standards which can be useful in the study of other writings as well' (Beardslee 1970: 3–4). Beardslee traces two lines of tradition from Aristotle in interpreting texts: that from the *Rhetoric*, in which form is seen as distinct from content, which may stand independently of it, and that from the *Poetics*, which tends to regard form as 'an essential part of the function of the work, and not as a separate, instrumental addition to the intellectual content'. Hammond (1983) bemoans the way in which biblical critics have concerned themselves with sources, with the processes of compilation, with historical facts 'behind' the text, and with the 'author'. Literary critics, on the other hand, are more subjective and intuitive, more geared towards interpretation and synthesis.

Gardner (1982: 35) drew attention to the classic understanding of humanity as *animal capax rationis*, and she suggested that this needs expansion by the term *capax reverentiae*, 'capable of feeling reverence and awe, of recognising excellence, of feeling a sense of freedom from the categories of space and time before what is beautiful, noble, or sublime, and desiring to celebrate, to give thanks, and to praise'. Gardner's primary concern is, of course, with the capacity of literature to evoke such a response, yet what she has to say is not without significance for the reading of the Bible. She also points (1982: 29) to the dangers of reading any text with a concern for immediate 'relevance', and insists upon the primacy of 'amusement, pleasure, enjoyment', which must have some affinity with Christian understandings of celebration. There follows upon this a secondary sense in which reading literature (to quote T.S. Eliot) 'has something to do with morals'. This is not the same as the 'inculcation of morals', but has rather to do with the sense in which literature 'strongly engages our moral sympathies, and tests our moral allegiances'.

Ephesians displays these same concerns. The primacy of celebration is evident, and celebration, for this writer, must issue in behaviour. Ephesians, as indeed all the texts which constitute our Bible, may be seen to contribute to the attempt (in Kavanagh's words) to 'thicken the meaning found in reality and increment that meaning with style' (1984: 47). To these insights may be added that of Steiner (1993), who notes the sense in which worshippers listening to a reading of the scriptures are involved in a corporate act of interpretation, which is akin to the task of translation. Steiner begins by drawing attention to the fact that, even when reading or hearing texts in one's own language, one is involved in a continuous process of translation: 'Any thorough reading of a text out of the past of one's own language and literature is a manifold act of interpretation. In the great majority of cases, this act is hardly performed or even consciously recognised. At best, the common reader will rely on what instant crutches footnotes or a glossary provide' (1993: 18), and again, 'When we read or hear any language statement from the past, be it Leviticus or last year's bestseller, we translate' (1993: 28).

This is particularly germane to the reading of the Bible, at a time when several scholars are coming to the view that the historical critical method has reached an impasse. Via remarked in his study of the parables (1967) that, while scholars such as Wilder had commented on the aesthetic nature of the parables, no one had treated them as objects of creative art in their own right. 'Today the future of the historical critical paradigm is a lively question' (Peterson 1978: 10).

Gardner and Eliot represented a particular strand in literary criticism. More recent – post-structuralist – readings of texts find the 'mystery' not beyond the text, but within it. Derrida (1974) asserts the primacy of texts, along with reading and writing. Taylor (1984) and Moore (1992) take these ideas further and construct an approach to texts which is playful and disconcerting when set against more traditional approaches. Ephesians is a piece of *writing* – part of a literary tradition, which has antecedents (contexts) and a continuing context (the worship of the church and the self-understanding of a society). It may be illegitimate to talk of the intention of the author, but the text clearly has an intention, and that is to persuade the readers of the truth of its message and the validity of its demands.

EPHESIANS AS HISTORY AND LITERATURE

This introductory chapter has set the background for a reading of the epistle. The success of the historical method since the rise of historical consciousness in the eighteenth century has brought about a shift in our culture's assumptions about history. The desire to establish 'what actually happened' historically has resulted in the recognition that certainty concerning historical questions is not possible. At the same time there has arisen an interest in how texts are to be approached in ways which take their *literary* features more seriously. The recognition of the context of worship in the development of the New Testament documents may provide a perspective on the function which biblical texts perform in the Christian community today: that is, not so much to provide information about the past, as to assist believing communities to meet with God. Such an emphasis inevitably entails such communities having their perspective, both on the world and on their behaviour in it, changed into something which makes sense alongside their religious commitment.

In deciding in this *Reading* against authorship by the apostle Paul himself, we have aligned ourselves with the majority of scholars of the modern era – and more about this will be said in the next chapter in our consideration of the figure of Paul. Moreover, a theory concerning the purpose of the epistle will emerge in the course of this *Reading*. However, we shall need to bear in mind that these historical concerns are to be held alongside the literary interests which arise in a reading of the epistle.

The structure of the epistle combines that of the hellenistic letter with that of Jewish letters. It begins with both a Benediction (1.3–14) and a Thanksgiving (1.15–2.22), and proceeds through a memorial to Paul (3.1–21) to an ethical exhortation (4.1–6.9). The epistle concludes with the image of the church as a soldier armed with God's own armour for the battle with evil (6.10–20). The language of the epistle is ambiguous and pleonastic, as is fitting for the context of worship for which the epistle was written. A particular feature of the language centres upon God's plan to 'sum up' all things in Christ. This is a rhetorical expression, and it is applied to the saving action of God by means of Christ. The life-setting of the epistle is the worship of the community, and this forms the context in which the epistle continues to have meaning.

The text highlights the implications of the restatement of Paul's gospel as the declaration of God's plan to unite the whole human race in the one body of Christ. The ethical implications of all this are spelled out in 4.1–6.9, with an ethic of unity which is built upon the teaching contained in the Benediction and Thanksgiving of 1–2. Finally, the image of the 'armour of God' in 6.10–20 will complete the epistle's task of re-stating the gospel while also celebrating the figure of Paul, whose position in the plan of God was so crucial to its vindication and success.

Chapter 2

The legacy of Paul

'Paul, an apostle of Jesus Christ ...' (1.1). The first word of the Epistle to the Ephesians presents the reader with the problem which was discussed in the previous chapter: how does the figure of Paul relate to the text of Ephesians? This is the 'problem' of pseudepigraphy: how can a religious text be written in the name of somebody else? Does that not compromise its claim to 'truth'? How does Ephesians, if pseudonymous, relate to the letters of Paul himself?

There is an extensive literature on the phenomenon of pseud-epigraphy in the ancient world, and the practice of pseudonymous writing in ancient Christian literature has given rise to much scholarly debate. For some, the very notion is unthinkable, since such a practice would amount to forgery. Von Rückert (1834) took this view, as did Guthrie (1964), who ruled out any possibility of the existence of pseudepigraphy in the New Testament at all. However, Guthrie was far too dependent upon the external testimony of the early church, which had an interest in naming as apostolic those documents which were in the process of becoming canonical (Evans 1971). Guthrie pays insufficient regard to the evidence of the documents themselves, and fails to discern the distinction between the kind of forgery in which the memory of the assumed writer is done no credit by the ascription of the pseudepigraphical work, and those cases of 'genuine' pseudepigraphy, in which the author wished to assert their indebtedness to the memory of the author whose name is used. Guthrie had too great an interest in preserving a dogmatic tradition of the 'authority' of the text, as though the admission of pseudonymity would call this into question. He did not reckon with the possibility that the text may have an intrinsic authority, regardless of its authorship, which led to its recognition as a document of 'holy scripture'.

PAUL AND PSEUDONYMITY

It is inevitable that Paul should figure quite heavily in any developed understanding of the gospel as it appeals to both Jews and Gentiles. It is clear from his own writings and from the Acts of the Apostles that he had been at the forefront of the Gentile mission. However, there is a further reason for such an emphasis on his place in the church's memory later in the first century. Barrett suggested (1974) that there may have been some sense in which Paul's death was discreditable to the church at the time. Paul was clearly a controversial character; he was in conflict with Peter at Antioch, according to Galatians 2, and with opponents at Corinth, according to 2 Corinthians 10–13. There was disagreement over the collection of money for the church at Jerusalem. There was also, possibly, dispute over christology; Barrett looks in this regard at the Pauline interpolations into early Christian hymns such as Romans 1, Philippians 2 and Colossians 1.

Barrett sets himself the question, how did the various controversies end in which Paul was involved? Surveying the controversies just mentioned, he observes that, with the death of Paul, the situation of the early church was transformed. In particular, he draws attention to the figures of Peter and James. In the case of Peter's death, he prefers a date in the time of Nero (54–68 AD); and in the case of James's, he considers the date derived from Josephus (*Antiquities* 20.200) of 62 AD as more probable than those derived from Eusebius (*Historia Ecclesiae* 2.23.18), of either 69 AD or 66/7 AD.

Barrett points out that the only reason for supposing that Paul's death was later than Peter's is the fact that Peter is mentioned first in 1 Clement 5.3, and this is hardly a sufficient reason. Paul journeyed to Jerusalem with the collection in 55 AD, the year before Festus took office. He consequently arrived in Rome in 56 or 57 AD. His two years under house arrest would take him to 58 or 59 AD. The question is, how did this house arrest end? According to the pastoral epistles, he was subsequently released, and engaged in further missionary activity in the East. According to 1 Clement, however, he travelled further west, reaching Spain. 1 Clement also records that he died 'as a result of jealousy', and the context indicates that he is speaking of Jews rather than of Romans.

Barrett also considers the question of the ending of the Acts of the Apostles. Making reference to 2 Corinthians 11.26, he suggests that, in the end, Jews were joined by Jewish Christians in bringing about Paul's downfall. He further suggests that James failed to show any support for him, noting that Acts 21–6 shows no sign of James acting on his behalf. Alternatively, it is possible that the expression 'as a result of strife' in 1 Clement is a fiction based upon Acts 3–5 and 12, which the writer had read. Barrett does admit the possibility, but does not take it seriously. Barrett suggests that Paul and James died first, leaving Peter to emerge as the dominant figure, the 'rock' upon which the church was to stand. This would explain the characteristics of the sub-apostolic period: neither 'Judaizing', that is, tending to insist on the ritual of circumcision and the observation of food laws, nor thoroughly 'Pauline', that is, with an emphasis on 'justification by faith' (perhaps because Paul was not properly understood).

Much of the rest of Barrett's argument about Pauline controversies is not of immediate interest to us, but he does comment, with regard to Ephesians, that it could not have been written when Jerusalem was still sponsoring an anti-Pauline mission; only when James and his community had ceased to exist would such an integration as that envisaged in Acts 15 have been possible.

A date for the Epistle to the Ephesians soon after the destruction of Jerusalem fits very well with the order of events as portrayed by Barrett. In such circumstances, the collection of Paul's letters could be regarded either as an act of expiation on the part of those who connived at his death, or, what is more likely, an act of piety on the part of his disciples. The Epistle to the Ephesians may then be read as an attempt to re-assert Paul's significance, now that his message had been vindicated by events.

A RATIONALE FOR PSEUDONYMITY

The Epistle to the Ephesians is therefore an early pseudepigraph, and it needs to be interpreted in the light of its antecedents in Jewish and Greek literature. Brox (1975) draws attention to the fact that, in ancient Israel, the writing of laws was ascribed to Moses, the composition of psalms to David and the creation of wise sayings to Solomon. Apocalyptic writers made extensive use of the names of ancient characters, including Daniel, Enoch, Ezra, Baruch, Moses, Abraham, Noah and Isaiah. Jewish writers also made use of non-Jewish names, as in the case of the Sibylline Oracles, and the Testament of Orpheus. Brox makes the point that, in Jewish tradition, pseudepigraphy has to be seen against the background of literary activity in which the individuality of an author plays a part akin to the generally recognized name which stands for a particular tradition. 'That is to say, one must take great care not to evaluate fictional authorship as a conscious programme of deception and forgery in a moral sense' (1975: 44).

Brox also discusses pseudepigraphy in Greek writing, beginning with Orphic traditions, and making reference also to the fact that the works of Hippocrates, Homer, Hesiod and Democritus all betray evidence of pseudonymity. There are several reasons for this in Greek literature. In some cases, later writers wanted to fill gaps in the knowledge about certain poets, or historical authors, and so created further writings in their name. The growth of Neo-platonism and Neo-pythagoreanism was largely due to the inventiveness of writers under the names of Plato and Aristotle (1975: 46). More specifically, pseudonymity was prevalent in epistolary literature, partly because letter writing lent itself to this treatment. Many examples stem from schools of rhetoric and are simply exercises in the imitation of style, but pseudonymous documents frequently found their way into the corpus of collected works of the person they set out to imitate. In some cases (Gudemann 1894) it has proved impossible to judge whether a work is authentic or not.

In a wide-ranging discussion of the phenomenon, Speyer (1971) isolates the practice of literary forgery from that of pseudepigraphy in general, on the basis that the latter may come about as a result of a variety of circumstances. First, students of rhetoric in the ancient world would set out deliberately to write speeches in the style of a particular orator. Second, in schools and libraries of hellenistic kingdoms, secretaries would be engaged upon the production of great volumes of written material; eventually, this was collected under the title of the ruler who sent it out. Third, philosophers and doctors gathered around them groups of students who frequently wrote treatises in the name of their patrons, as a sign of honour to them. Fourth, there was a kind of 'mythical', or genuine religious pseudepigraphy, in which the writer came eventually to be perceived as writing in the name of the gods. Speyer sees parallels of this in the way in which Yahweh often speaks in the first person in the Old Testament, especially in the mouth of Moses and the prophets, as well as in later apocalypticists. Finally, there existed a 'non-genuine' type of the genre, in which direct religious inspiration was lacking, and the writing degenerated into conscious fraud; this may be detected, he says, by a certain rigidity of style.

Turning to the more specific field of 'literary forgery', Speyer observes eight motives for the device of pseudonymity, in which there must be some intention to deceive.

1   The first is the desire to increase the level of respect in which the writing is held. There were two preconditions for this type of pseudepigraphy: the writer's sense of his own inferiority, and his recognition of a 'canon' of names of famous writers. In the case of Greek literature, there was a long tradition of famous writers from Homer onwards, and the list inevitably grew throughout the years of Greek civilization, with significant characters in the fields of religion, poetry and the sciences. Speyer points out that the first precondition, the feeling of inferiority, is bound to no particular time, but can be present whenever a culture is conscious of being a 'later epoch' in the course of history, as was the case with both hellenistic and imperial Roman society. This motive would differ little from Speyer's second, and it has links with others of the eight. However, he retains it as a distinct category, since other factors are also present in the remaining seven.

2   The second motive is the desire to achieve a particular effect, usually, though not exclusively, of an aesthetic kind, and Speyer refers to philosophical and literary examples, with parallels from the fine arts. Thus Phaedrus, the fabulist (Prologue 1–9), justifies his making use of the name of Aesop by comparing his practice to that of a sculptor who signed his work with the name of Praxiteles.

3   The third motive is the desire for financial gain. This is traceable to the desire on the part of many hellenistic rulers to own prestigious libraries, especially those in Alexandria and Pergamum (Gudemann 1894: 62, 73).

4   The fourth motive is that of personal animosity. An example is the story told of Odysseus's writing under the name of Priam to Palamedes in order to portray the former as a traitor. Speyer refers also to invectives written under false names in the context of the strife which characterized the Roman republic, and to the case of Apuleius (*Apology* 82.4), whose opponents accused him of sorcery, because he succeeded in marrying a rich widow, Pudentilla, who was several years older than himself. By way of defence, he laid before the court a letter from Pudentilla to her son. He was able to

demonstrate that a particular offending passage in it was an insertion, quite out of context, and the sense of the letter as a whole had been misrepresented.

5   The fifth motive is the need or desire to complete or supplement existing tradition. This is frequently the case with tradition which is defective in some way, and which the authorities wish to use to establish or create, for example, the actually or allegedly ancient rights of a sanctuary or of a state, or to increase the reputation of a famous person, place, sanctuary or state, or to give authority to changes in the areas of religion, morality or law by means of authoritative witness from the past. Orphic traditions fall into this category, and Dionysius of Halicarnassus (*De Thucydide* 23) says of prose writers prior to Thucydides, 'Of the majority no writings remain, and of the books still extant, not all are to be regarded as genuine.'

6   The sixth motive is the defence of philosophical and other kinds of teaching. Some pseudepigrapha under this heading are the result of animosity, while some are designed to honour the master; the Pseudopythagorica come under this heading, diverse though they are (Burkert 1961).

7   The seventh motive is that which serves political or patriotic ends. Many of these are of a religious nature, consisting of oracles which elaborate or interpret myths with a political intention (Speyer 1971: 142–5).

8   Finally, Speyer notes a religious motive. In spite of philosophy, sophism, enlightenment and hellenistic wisdom, the ancient world was bound to religion. As he showed in his seventh category of motive, one element of this religion was the service of political ends, such as that which made Alexander the Great a son of the gods, or in which Alexander himself commended the oriental god–kings to the Greeks (Jacoby 1923–54: 659). A further aim is the desire of religious places and sanctuaries to obtain or retain the right of asylum (as in Tacitus, *Annals* 3.60.3). Others serve to heighten the reputation of religious prophets and magicians; yet others to further the purposes of religious propaganda (Weinreich 1969: 410.43; *Jahrbuch für Antike und Christentum* 8/9 1965/6: 101; Jaeger 1953: 74f.) Later in the Christian centuries, pseudepigraphical works against Christianity appeared. With its increasing popularity and eventual adoption as the official religion of the Empire, it became possible to attack Christianity only under cloak of pseudonymity.

In the light of this discussion, it is clear that the motives of the writer of the Epistle to the Ephesians may be akin to several, though not all, of those which Speyer examines. Ephesians evidently succeeded in gaining recognition, though it is not possible to know whether its original intentions succeeded. Clearly there was no thought of financial gain, and the idea of animosity must also be ruled out; there is no sign of any real polemic in the letter.

There is, however, evidence of a clear desire to supplement a religious tradition, which here was Christian and, especially, Pauline. The writer consciously looks back (2.20; 3.5) to 'the holy apostles and prophets' and, before them, to the 'chief corner-stone, Christ Jesus himself'. He elaborates his own understanding of the relationship between Jews and Gentiles in the church, in a development of Paul's own. The fifth, sixth and eighth motives therefore coalesce in the epistle's concern both to develop Pauline tradition and to urge a theme of teaching which is a legitimate development of Paul's. This is the theological significance, within the plan of God, of the destruction of Jerusalem as a sequel to the crucifixion and resurrection of Christ, and is elaborated in Ephesians 2.

To this analysis of pseudepigraphical literature in Graeco-Roman culture may perhaps be added the contribution of the Jewish religious pseudepigraphical tradition. Russell (1971) suggests that there were four elements at work in the development of pseud-epigraphical apocalyptic writings. First, at the time at which the literature began to appear, it would have been dangerous for the true authors to put their own names to their work, for fear of persecution. Second, there was the glamour of antiquity: the notion that all that was of value must have come to be or have taken place in the long distant past. Third, there was the idea that authority resided in ancient figures, since the canon of scripture was thought to have been closed with the work of Ezra in the third century BC. Fourth, Russell refers to quite practical and fortuitous reasons, especially in the case of the Book of Daniel; stories about Daniel gradually came to be linked with apocalyptic visions which were ascribed to him.

Russell points out that there was no intention to deceive in any morally reprehensible sense; the Hebrew concept of 'corporate personality' meant that the writers of apocalyptic literature per-ceived themselves not as original creators of literary works, but as inheritors and interpreters of a religious tradition which could be traced to the ancient figure whose name it bore, such as Moses, Enoch, Ezra and Daniel. Mowinkel had seen this as a precursor of the concept of the 'patron saint'. In addition, there were two other factors, the idea of the contemporaneity of the past with the present (Russell 1971: 205ff.) and the concept of the name as an extension of the personality.

This pseudepigraphical tradition clearly continued within Judaism and in early Christianity. While nobody would say that Ephesians was apocalyptic, it nevertheless deals with the ultimate goal of creation. There are further parallels between the pseudepigraphical writing of Ephesians and that of apocalyptic literature, however. While it is unlikely that the writer was in any kind of danger, or that Ephesians was written specifically for inclusion in a canon of Paul's letters, Russell's other two points remain forceful: there was evidently a great regard for the past and for authoritative figures from the past; and the writer evidently saw himself as continuing and interpreting a tradition, hence his extensive use of the letters of Paul.

CONSTRUCTING PAUL

How is Ephesians to be read in the light of this discussion? From the standpoint of Jewish pseudepigraphy, we can see how Ephesians inherits and interprets a religious tradition, and constructs Paul as a significant, authoritative figure of the past. It is also true to say that Ephesians viewed the past as particularly authoritative. Pauline tradition was not a feature of the *distant* past, but, for early Christian writers, the supremely significant event of the past was the life, death and resurrection of Jesus, who was believed to be the Christ, which ushers in the end of history. For Ephesians, as in other instances of New Testament pseudepigraphy, this past developed with the ministry of the apostles and the founding of the churches, which soon came to be seen as the founding of the one church. Recent though these events may have been, comparatively speaking, they were still authoritative because they were the eschatological actions of God.

When the Jewish tradition is taken together with that of Greek writers, an even clearer picture emerges. Reference has already been made to the desire of Ephesians to gain authority and recognition for its teaching, and to develop Pauline tradition (see p.27 above). The authority of the past is understood in a way

similar to that derived from Jewish tradition. Perhaps most significantly, however, is the element of religious motive, in which many
of these elements meet. This is clearly the case with both Jewish
pseudepigraphy in the apocalyptic tradition, and with the desire
in that strand of Greek pseudepigraphical literature both to
heighten the reputation of religious figures and to propagate
religious teaching.

All this is significant because a closer reading of Ephesians as a
pseudepigraph underlines the nature of the letter as primarily
religious. The epistle is concerned with the church's self-
understanding, and the importance of Paul is that he is the
mediator of this religious tradition. The liturgical atmosphere of
the letter, particularly its opening with a Benediction in 1.3–14
and its development through a Thanksgiving prayer in 1.15–2.22,
underline this intention. The opening Benediction states that all
things are the object of the divine 'summing up' in Christ; all
things, that is, in heaven and on earth. In Ephesians 2, the writer
goes on to expound the meaning of this 'in heaven' and 'on
earth'. In heaven it means the overcoming of the powers inimical
to God, and which separate humanity from God (2.1–10), while
on earth it means the end of the hostility between Israel and the
Gentiles (2.11–22).

Thus in the placing side by side of Benediction and Thanksgiving, there is emphasis on the religious nature of the writing,
which is expressed in terms of public liturgy and petition, and in
the unfolding of the meaning of the 'summing up' there is an
insistence on the importance of the content of the religious
understanding of events which the writer wishes to convey. The
epistle expresses a religious understanding of the connection
between the death of Christ and the destruction of the Temple.
The effect of this had been that the dividing fence between the
Court of the Gentiles and the Court of Israel was broken down.
Ephesians is an interpretation of this event. The death of Christ
had been perceived by Paul as having implications for the Gentiles,
and the destruction of the Temple is seen as, in some sense,
underlining those implications and vindicating the apostle.

How then is Paul understood in this epistle? The fact of its
pseudonymity makes the reading of Ephesians 3 particularly interesting. As the chapter begins, 'For this reason, I Paul, the prisoner
of the Lord for you Gentiles' (3.1), it looks as though the writer is
about to embark upon the kind of moral exhortation which does,

in fact, begin in 4.1. In 3.1–13 the writer makes a total of seven points as he depicts the apostle reacting in wonder to his own exposition of God's plan for the salvation of all who believe, and the incorporation of Gentiles along with Israel in the church. What follows in Ephesians 3, then, is not so much a digression from the main thrust of the epistle, but rather a conscious device which draws attention to the person of Paul, and especially his status as an apostle to the Gentiles. It regards him as one privileged to perceive the mystery of the gospel, and his call to preach it is a mark of divine favour (3.2–3). However, one is still left wondering why the writer devotes twelve verses to an exposition of Paul's status. In Ephesians 3, much attention is paid to Paul's sufferings, which are said to be 'on behalf of' the Gentiles. The writer evidently believes that, in some sense, Paul's sufferings were, like his Master's, vicarious and expiatory. In Colossians 1.24 Paul himself makes reference to his own 'making up whatever may be lacking in the sufferings of Christ'.

Houlden (1977) sees this passage (3.1–13) as an assertion of Paul's vocation to be 'God's chosen instrument to bring about the Gentiles' participation in the redeemed community'. It underlines Paul's authority, albeit that of service and suffering, like Christ's, and this adds force to the writer's claim that, as Paul is the apostle to the Gentiles, the church should look to Paul as the basis for unity. Already, in his lifetime, Paul's apostolate had been embarrassed by the activity of others, and so his Christ-given relationship to all the Gentile congregations, including those not founded by him, needed asserting. However, Houlden does not spell out in what circumstances that assertion might have been necessary. Neither is the assertion of Paul's authority as polemical as Houlden suggests.

The following analysis of the chapter will seek to show how it fits in with the understanding of the epistle adopted in this *Reading*. First, the writer refers to Paul's suffering – 'I, Paul, the prisoner of the Lord for you Gentiles' (3.1). Paul refers to himself in Philemon 1.9 as 'a prisoner of Christ Jesus', and the expression recurs in 2 Timothy 1.8. Most of the commentators agree that 'prisoner' is a word play. Paul is portrayed as in prison for the sake of the Christ, certainly, but he is also captive to Christ – 'for you Gentiles'. It is clear from such passages as 2 Corinthians 11.23ff. that Paul suffered persecution of various kinds during his own lifetime, but, as has been indicated above, following the argument advanced by Barrett, the text also perhaps indicates the possibility that Paul's life came to an end in such a way, and in such circumstances, that it became possible with hindsight to depict those sufferings as vicarious or representative.

Second, Paul is the recipient of revelation: 'if, indeed, you have heard of the dispensation of the grace of God which was given to me for you, that the mystery was made known to me by revelation, as I formerly wrote to you briefly' (3.2–3). Abbott (1897) notes that the expression 'if you have heard' indicates that the writer knows that the readers were not themselves hearers of Paul's own teaching and instruction. Since Paul is not the author of the epistle, this is perhaps to be regarded as the writer's way of introducing the readers to the wonder of the grace of God in granting Paul his special commission to preach the gospel to the Gentiles. In the double absence of Paul, the revelation is both carried and comes to birth in the text of Ephesians.

God revealed to Paul his universal plan, and the emphasis on revelation, which is reminiscent of Galatians 1.12, underlines the divine initiative in Paul's vocation and mission. The gospel is a 'mystery' – perhaps a 'secret' – in that it was previously hidden, but it has now been made known in the fact of Paul's preaching and in the text of the epistle. The writer indicates that Paul's own letters teach what Paul preached – 'as I have written to you briefly' – and that what he preached 'was not known by former generations' (3.5). It seems likely that Paul himself would have made some reference here to what could be known of the gospel in the scriptures (cf. Romans 1). The other 'holy apostles and prophets' share also in this revelation, so Paul is retrospectively equated with them – as he himself had insisted, for example, in Galatians 2.

The third point which the writer makes re-emphasizes the content of the 'mystery' which has just been expounded in the latter part of Ephesians 2: the Gentiles have an equal share with Israel in the promises which centre in Christ; those who formerly were alienated from Israel have now been brought near and made both sharers in its polity and fellow-heirs of the Messianic promises; 'that the Gentiles should be made fellow inheritors, members of the same body and partakers together of the promise in Christ Jesus through the gospel' (3.6). The three words which emphasize the new state of affairs – 'fellow inheritors, members of the same body and partakers together' – have in Greek the same prefix, *sun-*, as the verbs in 2.5–6, 'made us alive together, raised us up together, made us sit together'. The sharing of the Gentiles in the gospel is to do with inheritance, corporateness and participation. The inheritance is the same as Israel's, the corporate body is the body of Christ, and the Gentiles' participation is in the eschatological promise of a Messiah which was made to Israel, the people of God.

The fourth point is the reiteration of Paul's vocation to proclaim to the Gentiles these 'unfathomable riches' of Christ (3.8). The use of the adjective 'unfathomable' echoes Romans 11.33, 'O the depths of the riches and wisdom and knowledge of God! How unsearchable are his judgments and how unfathomable his ways!', and the theme is similar. Paul is here to be regarded as the 'servant' of the gospel, as he is in his own words in 2 Corinthians 11.23. It is perhaps worth noting at this point that, if M. Barth (1960, 1974), Fischer (1973) and Meyer (1977) were correct in their understanding of Ephesians as concerned primarily with mission, this is the point at which one might expect some kind of exhortation to continue that mission – but there is none. What there is, is a focus upon the person of Paul, who was called by God. His humility – 'the least of all the saints' (3.8) – underlines the wisdom and grace of God in calling him; if Barrett is correct in suggesting that some Christians played a part in Paul's downfall and death, the passage has a certain pathos in its recollection of the apostle's memory, and this adds weight to the ethical material which is to follow.

The fifth point is that the saving act of God has cosmic implications – 'that the manifold wisdom of God might now be made known through the church to the principalities and powers in the heavenlies. This was according to the eternal purpose which he realized in Christ Jesus our Lord' (3.10–11). Christ has been portrayed as victorious over the powers in the first half of Ephesians 2, and the enmity between Israel and the Gentiles is shown to be abolished in the second half of the chapter. The Christian community is subsequently (4.13; 6.10ff.) called upon to stand its ground against the attacks of the powers as it physically grows up through them to the full stature of Christ. The 'principalities and powers' have been made aware of what is happening to them in accordance with God's plan, since their defeat by the resurrection is made plain by the preaching of the gospel and the growth of the body of Christ.

The sixth point is a reminder to the readers that, as a result of Paul's preaching of the gospel, they all experience 'boldness and access in confidence to God through faith'. This is an echo of Paul's teaching in Romans 5.2, and the readers of Ephesians are clearly expected to share this experience.

Finally, reference is made again to the apostle's sufferings, which lead the writer into prayer. This is not fortuitous, for here is an understanding of prayer which relates it closely to conflict and suffering (Williams 1979: 4–21). This was so in the case of Jesus, and it is also for Paul, so this is how it is to be for the continuing community, as the discussion of Ephesians 6.10ff. in chapter 8 below makes clear. In the prayer of 3.14–19, the writer depicts Paul as the typical person of prayer. Paul is portrayed as desiring that the community, made up of Jew and Gentile, may be strengthened to perceive yet greater depths of love among themselves, as they have known the love of Christ, which passes knowledge. This provides the background for expressing the hope that they will be 'filled with God's fulness', which is in anticipation of Christ's fulness in 4.13. The meaning of this is to be expounded at the end of the epistle.

The passage is thus concerned with something very much within the life of the church, and it also highlights the function of the text. Reflection upon the significance of Paul gives rise to an understanding of the event of Christ within the life of humanity which cuts across the barrier of spiritual powers that separates humankind from God, and that holds apart the two groups of humanity, Jew and Gentile. The epistle does not urge its readers to emulate Paul in his apostolic, or missionary, zeal: it invites them to recognize why they are what they are, and to perceive the central position of Paul in this as God's servant. It invites them to consider the ways of God: Paul, the one who is the typical prisoner of Christ for the sake of the Gentiles, is also the typical person of prayer. The readers of this meditation are to perceive both its truth and its implications.

It is hardly surprising that the apostle Paul should figure so prominently in such an understanding. It was he, in particular, who had been the foundation of the Gentile mission. Moreover, if Barrett is right in thinking that Paul's death brought some discredit to the church, then Ephesians may well be an attempt to reassert Paul's significance now that his message had been vindicated by events. The amount of attention paid to Paul's sufferings, which are said to be 'on behalf of' the Gentiles (3.1), suggests that the readers are to take very seriously the writer's estimate of Paul. Ephesians is a conscious piece of religious writing. In it a follower of Paul who wishes to rehabilitate him and reinterpret his message, in a day when events have vindicated his preaching, sets out an original insight into the action of God. The basis of the subsequent moral exhortation is thereby underlined. There is a connection between the action of God in Christ, the significance of Paul and the 'worthy walk' to which believers are called. Ephesians is the attempt to persuade the readers of this connection and to urge them to act in a certain way. It has, therefore, a *rhetorical* function, for rhetoric is the art of persuasion. In a particular way in Ephesians rhetoric comes to the service of theology.

Chapter 3

Summing up

After our jump ahead to a reading of Ephesians 3 in order to fill out the verbal picture which is presented of Paul, we return now to the beginning of the epistle and the Benediction which opens it (1.3–10). We observed at the end of the previous chapter that rhetoric has come to the service of theology in Ephesians. Perhaps, rather, both theology and rhetoric come to be seen as mutually instructive, for 'rhetoric' is enhanced and broadened by the juxtaposition of theology, just as its definition is widened by Eagleton (1983), in his observation that all texts may be explained in the light of their *persuasive* effect. First, Ephesians sets out to *1* persuade its readers of a distinctive understanding of the gospel and of a particular way of life to be lived in accordance with it. Second, it seeks to do this by means of the concept of 'summing *2* up', which has its roots, though not its total semantic thrust, as we shall see, in the field of rhetoric.

God's eternal plan for the world, according to Ephesians 1.10, is '*to sum up* all things in Christ'. The Greek word for 'to sum up' is *anakephalaiôsasthai*, and it is a striking term to use for God's action *✳* in Christ. It is used in only one other place in the New Testament, in Romans 13.9: 'And if there is any other commandment, it *is summed up* in this; you shall love your neighbour as yourself.' In Romans, Paul is bringing the individual commands of the Torah under one, more inclusive, command; there is evidence of Rabbis also attempting this (Strack and Billerbeck 1922–61, III: 106). This chapter takes a technical look at this word, and then sets it in the context of the Benediction in which it occurs.

A WORD STUDY

We need to note first that *anakephalaiôsis* (the noun cognate with
the verb) subsequently became a technical term in the theology of
St Irenaeus of Lyon in the second century AD. He found the word
in Ephesians a useful counterblast to the opinions of Gnostics, who
wished to deny the identity of the God who was creator of all things
and the God who redeemed the world in Christ. His doctrine of
'recapitulation' argued that Christ, in his incarnation, 'recap-
itulated' the story of Adam (*Adversus Haereses* 5.21.1), thus proving
the unity of God with the created world of humanity. According to
Irenaeus, Christ repeated Adam's story but, instead of yielding to
temptation, resisted it and so brought about the salvation of the
world (Lawson 1948: 144).

From this idea Irenaeus derived an understanding of the comprehensive nature of Christian salvation. Christ, as the Son of God,
pre-existent with the Father, 'summed up' in his incarnate self the
long line of the human race, 'that we might recover in Christ Jesus
what in Adam we lost, namely, the state of being in the image and
likeness of God' (*Adversus Haereses* 3.18.1). Following the text of
Ephesians, Irenaeus extended this 'recapitulation' or 'summing
up' beyond the realm of humanity to 'all things':

> that, as in things above the heavens and in the spiritual and
> invisible world the word of God is supreme, so in the visible and
> physical realm he may have the pre-eminence, taking to himself
> the primacy and appointing himself head of the church, that he
> may 'draw all things to himself' in due time.
>
> (*Adversus Haereses* 3.16.6)

For Irenaeus, 'summing up' is the work of salvation, the activity of
Christ in reversing the 'fall' of Adam. In this 'summing up', God
brings together, or unites, all things in Christ, and Christ repeats,
or re-enacts, human history.

However, we need to ask to what extent is this meaning present
in the text of Ephesians, where the reference would appear to be
more 'eschatological' and ecclesiological than in Irenaeus? Also,
are there any other semantic possibilities? We need to get behind
this particular set of doctrines in order to understand the word in
this passage in the New Testament. In classical Greek the verb 'to
sum up' is found in rhetorical textbooks. A fragment of Aristotle,
for example, says, 'the tasks of rhetoric are . . . to preface the case

in such a way as to arouse the goodwill of one's hearers, to set it out in detail so that they will believe it, to work hard at making it clear, and *to sum up* so as to make recollection easy for them' (Diels 1934–54: 123.1499a.33). Similarly, Dionysius of Halicarnassus, speaking of the rhetorical style of Lysias, says (*De Lysia* 9), 'when summing up, his style is lax and abrupt.' These examples illustrate Quintilian's observation (*Institutio Orationis* 6.1.1), 'the setting out and gathering together of points, which in Greek is called "summing up", and by certain Latin authors *enumeratio*, serves both to refresh the memory of the judge and at the same time to set the whole case before him.' The occurrence of the word ✳ *anakephalaiôsis* in these rhetorical contexts combines the two elements of 'repetition' and 'drawing together'. The 'summing up' of a list of commandments, or the points in a detailed argument by a politician or an advocate, may be said both to restate in shorter form and to unite in a briefer compass the disparate elements of what has preceded it.

The one occurrence of the word 'to sum up' in the Greek Bible is in Psalm 71.20 (MT Psalm 72) in the versions of Theodotion and the Quinta. Here the meaning is simply 'to come to an end'. The Septuagint and Aquila's version use different synonyms. Alongside this may be set its use in the *Epistle of Barnabas* 5.11, where the incarnation of the Son of God is said to have taken place 'in order that he might finally bring about the end of sins'; the verb is transitive and has 'the end' as its object. This introduces a further level of meaning in the word, that of 'to come (or be brought) to a conclusion', as distinct from 'to sum up'. This is not out of place in the context in which it occurs in Ephesians 1.10. The title 'Christ' is itself eschatological, in that the 'Messiah' is a figure who appears 'at the end of time', the liturgical atmosphere of 1.3–14 is one of fulfilment, and the *anakephalaiôsis* is referred to as the 'economy of the fulness of times'. The writer is clearly saying that, in some sense, ✳ 'all things' are brought to a conclusion in Christ.

Readers unfamiliar with Greek will perhaps allow a brief but necessary diversion through two and a half words in the original language, in order to clarify what we are discussing. The Greek verb in Ephesians 1.10, *anakephalaiôsasthai*, which is translated 'to sum up', is comprised of a number of lexical elements. These are (a) the noun *kephalaion*, which is derived from (b) the noun *kephalê*, and (c) the prefix *ana-*. A brief look at these will assist our understanding of the word in the context in which it appears in Ephesians.

kephalaion

The word *kephalaion* is primarily an adjective meaning 'things pertaining to the head'. As a noun it can be a synonym for 'head', but with diminutive force, and it is sometimes used as a metonym. Callias, the fifth-century BC comic writer, used it of 'heads of fish' (Callias, *Cycl.* 5.1), and there are examples of its being used of children and vegetables (Aristophanes, *Clouds* 981). It may also be used for 'head', in the sense of 'chief', when applied to a person. For instance, Plutarch (*Life of Pericles* 3) preserves a fragment of a comedy by Eupolis, in which Pericles is referred to as 'head of all (who have been brought up from) the underworld', and *Lucian* 14 speaks of Plato, Chrysippus and Aristotle as 'the real directors of my studies' (cf. Liddell and Scott 1864 *s.v. kephalaion*).

This last example may, on the other hand, be evidence for what is the most common meaning of *kephalaion*, namely, the 'main point', in a literary or rhetorical sense, as, for example, in Plato *Leges* 643c, 'the main point of education is proper upbringing'. A further example is found in Isocrates, in *Oratores Attici* 39d, 'the main point of what we have said'. Thus, again, Quintilian is able to state (*Institutio Orationis* 3.11.27), 'as we use it when we say, "it is the head of the whole matter"', or, as Menander says, "... generally speaking, though, anything which is to be demonstrated will be a 'head', but with varying degrees of importance."' In the New Testament this use of *kephalaion* is to be found in Hebrews 8.1, 'the main point of what we are saying'.

The idea of 'main' or 'chief' is also present in Demosthenes in such expressions as 'the crowning act of wrong' (*Against Aphobus* 815.6), or 'with these two actions he crowned all his misdeeds' (*Against Meidias* 520.27). This would correspond with the idea of 'rule' or 'supremacy', in so far as a 'main point' takes precedence over others, although the notion of 'bringing together' or 'uniting' is never far away. Hence *kephalaion* is to be regarded as meaning 'crowning act' in these instances. The word may also have financial or commercial significance and mean 'principal' or 'capital', as opposed to interest or income (Plato, *Leges* 742c and Demosthenes, *Olynthiac* II.27.10).

kephalê

As has been hinted earlier, however, it is possible that Ephesians intends the verb *anakephalaiôsasthai* to be understood in the light not only of *kephalaion*, which obviously underlies it, but also of *kephalê*, which possibly does. This word occurs four times in Ephesians: 'and he has put all things under his feet and has made him head over all things for the church' (1.22); 'Rather, speaking the truth in love, we are to grow up in every way into him who is the head, into Christ' (4.15); 'for the husband is head of the wife as Christ is the head of the church, his body, and is himself its Saviour' (5.23, twice).

The overwhelming majority of scholars have understood the meaning of *kephalê* in Ephesians to be 'head' in the sense of 'ruler', and this is the chief meaning of the metaphor in English. Abbott (1897: 34) entitled his section on Ephesians 1.20–3, 'The Supremacy of Christ'. Barth (1974: 183) maintained that the basic meaning was 'thoroughly biblical', namely 'ruler', with the emphasis on authority. Howard (1974) sought to establish the primacy of the idea of 'ruler' by arguing that the author of Ephesians consistently juxtaposes 'head' with 'feet' rather than with 'body'; the writer's concern, derived from his understanding of Psalm 8.6, was the cosmic rule of Christ. Schlier (1963: 89) maintained that Christ's headship is his sovereign rule over the cosmos.

The emphasis of all these scholars, then, is on the role of Christ as 'ruler'. However, this has little support in secular Greek literature. Moreover, it is surprising that so little attention has been paid to Bedale's article (1954) on the meaning of *kephalê* in the Pauline corpus. He argues that the word underwent an extension of meaning through its use in the Septuagint, as a result of its association in the minds of readers of the Greek Bible with other words used to translate the Hebrew *rosh*. Bedale points out that *rosh* can mean two things: (a) 'head', in the literal, anatomical sense, and thus as a metonym for 'man', as in Judges 5.30 etc., and 'sum' or 'total', as in Numbers 1.2; or (b) 'first' or 'beginning', for example, of the night watch (Judges 7.19) or in the phrase 'from the beginning' (Proverbs 8.23), though *reshith* is the more common word in the second instance.

Some difficulty may be found in applying Bedale's findings to the translation of the word *kephalê* in every instance of its use in the New Testament, but these are not insuperable. His overall case is convincing, and provides a clue to the extent of the possible meanings of *kephalê* not only in Paul, but also in other writers in the same theological tradition; in fact, to translate *kephalê* as 'head' in the sense of 'beginning' or 'source' makes very good sense of several passages in Ephesians.

It is a little strange, then, that Bedale himself excludes Ephesians 1.22 from his discussion of the meaning of *kephalê*. 'It is possible', he says of this verse, 'in view of the context, that it is the "overlordship" of Christ that is stressed' (1954: 214). In this passage the Greek expression which is frequently translated 'over all' is more appropriately understood as 'above all' or 'supremely', and the words 'to the church' should be translated as 'for the church'. The following translation is then the most appropriate: 'and, above all, he has given him as the beginning for the church'. This makes very good sense, both of the text and of its context.

The prefix '*ana-*'

Finally, what of the prefix '*ana-*'? A study of its usage in the New Testament reveals that it has a range of four possible meanings.

1 The first is a 'directional' sense, for those instances where some movement upwards is denoted, e.g. *anabibazô* 'to bring up', 'to pull up'; *anakathizô* 'to sit upright'; *anakuptô* 'to raise oneself', 'to straighten'; *anapempô* 'to send up' (of prayers, to heaven); *anapedaô* 'to jump up', 'to stand up', and so on;

2 The second is a 'repetitive' sense, indicating either repetition or return to a previous state. In this group may be included *anablepô* 'to regain sight' (in classical writers this verb was more directional, 'to look up'); *anagennaô* 'to beget again' (in 1 Pet 1.3); *anakainizô* 'to renew', and so on;

3 The third is an 'intensive' sense, such as *anastenazô* 'to sigh deeply', 'to lament', as an intensive form of *stenazô* 'to groan', 'to bewail'; *anapêros* 'crippled', as an intensive form of *pêros* 'weakened', 'disabled'; *anatomê* 'mutilation', for *tomê* 'cutting', 'hewing'; *anaphoneô* 'to call out', for *phoneô* 'to sound', 'to make a sound';

4 The fourth is a 'stylistic' sense, in which the prefix appears to have little or no denotative significance, but where it is more affective in meaning, such as *anangellô* 'to announce', 'to proclaim', which differs in meaning little from *angellô*; or *anadechomai* 'to receive', which differs from *dechomai* only in its 'social' overtones (for the receiving of guests, etc.) Similarly *anagraphô* 'to register', is 'to write' in defined social contexts.

Which of these possible senses of the prefix *ana-* is to be included in the meaning of *anakephalaiôsis* in Ephesians 1.10? The first, 'directional', sense applies metaphorically in the basic rhetorical sense of 'summing *up*'. If there is a 'financial' meaning implied in the metaphor, it is intriguing to note (Hanson 1946: 123) that it was customary for columns of figures to be totalled from the bottom to the top. In a metaphorical sense also it may be taken with the second of the possibilities arising out of the earlier discussion of *kephalaion*, namely 'rule' or 'supremacy'; it would then have a sense similar to that of the 'intensive' meaning, underlining the head's authority. The second, 'repetitive', meaning of the prefix may be taken (a) with that sense of *anakephalaiôsis* which denotes 're-enactment' or 'repetition'; (b) with the sense which denotes 'bringing together', or 'uniting', in the sense of 'restoring an original unity'; or (c) with the sense that denotes 'beginning again'. The third and fourth meanings, 'intensive' and 'stylistic', appeal largely on the grounds of the pleonastic nature of the language of Ephesians as a whole. Such an interpretation may linked with 'rule', 'supremacy' or 'conclusion' as senses of the noun.

Conclusion

There exists therefore a considerable breadth of meaning for the verb *anakephalaiôsasthai*, and the possibilities may be set out as follows:

1 'to re-enact, to repeat'
2 'to sum up'
3 'to rule'
4 'to unite'
5 'to bring to a conclusion, to crown'
6 'to start again'.

Most commentators choose between the possibilities as they see them, opt for one meaning, and reject the others. An alternative to this procedure would be to recognize the pleonastic and allusive style of Ephesians, and say that the whole range of senses plays some part in the meaning of this word. Such a solution, although seeming to evade the issue, in fact faces the linguistic evidence more squarely. The language of the epistle is florid and ambiguous; this is due to the liturgical atmosphere in which it is set. It reflects, in addition, the religious nature of the total vision of the church and of the gospel to which the epistle gives expression. The idea of 'summing up' is in keeping with the eschatological tone of the Benediction. The idea of 'rule' is quite appropriate, in the context of the lordship of Christ, and that of 'uniting' anticipates what the writer later says in the context of Israel and the Gentiles, walking worthy, the marriage imagery and the armour of God. The notion of 'bringing to a conclusion' is also appropriate in the eschatological context; that of 'starting again' recalls the Adamic imagery to be found in the 'perfect man' of Ephesians 4.13, in the marriage imagery in Ephesians 5 and in the passage concerning the armour of God (6.10–20). This conclusion suggests that the rest of the epistle should be examined more closely with a view to discovering how the various meanings are held together.

THE BENEDICTION

The examination of the rest of the epistle must begin with a look at the context in which the language of 'summing up' is introduced. This brings us to a consideration of the Benediction, and we need to be aware of both its structure and its content, for the former is the expression of the latter. The Benediction is a particular form of prayer in Jewish tradition, which takes its Hebrew name *berakah* (plural, *berakoth*) from the opening word, which means 'blessed'. The Berakah is a distinctive feature of Jewish worship, and its antecedents are to be found in various strata of Hebrew scriptures and Rabbinic writing. Its use here is evidence both of the liturgical setting of Ephesians and of Jewish influence upon early Christian forms of worship.

The earliest forms of the Benediction are discussed by Kirby in his study of the theology of the letter to the Ephesians (1968: 84ff.). He argues that the Benediction was originally an individual prayer, arising 'out of a situation where some amazing thing has happened and one of the persons involved expresses his amazement at the goodness of God', such as in Genesis 24, when Abraham's servant finds a wife for Isaac. Another such example is that to be found on the lips of Jethro, when told of the people of Israel's deliverance from Egypt in Exodus 18.10, or that of King Hiram of Tyre on hearing from Solomon in 1 Kings 5.7; and in Psalm 66.20 an unknown worshipper in the Temple has his prayers answered and blesses God for this.

Subsequently, according to Kirby, a corporate context for the

Benediction arose, in which God is celebrated as the Creator and Redeemer of his people, as in Genesis 14.19, where Melchizedek invokes a blessing on Abraham from 'God Most High, Maker of all things' and blesses God, 'who has delivered your enemies into your hand.' In 1 Kings 8.14–21, at Solomon's dedication of the Temple, the Benediction is no longer individual, but cultic and corporate, as in Nehemiah 9.5 and Psalm 105. Other 'third person' Benedictions (those in which God is not directly addressed, but referred to by means either of a relative pronoun or of a participle) are to be found in Psalm 143.1, Tobit 13.1 and Genesis 9.26. They have as their basis an act of God (cf. Psalm 143.1, 1 Maccabees 4.30, 2 Maccabees 15.34 and Psalms of Solomon 6.6) or the miraculous intervention of God (cf. Psalm 27.6, Daniel 3.51, Tobit 13.1, 1 Maccabees 4.24,30, 2 Maccabees 3.30, 15.34.). This is the case also in the New Testament Benedictions to be found in Luke 1.68, 2 Corinthians 1.3 and 1 Peter 1.3.

Kirby's suggestion that the Benediction was originally an individual prayer needs to be handled carefully, however. Societies such as ancient Israel and many non-Western communities today understand very differently the relationship between the individual and the community. The occurrence of Berakoth within the liturgical reading of the scriptures focuses the attention of the hearers upon the acts of God, which are all to do with the salvation-story of Israel, first in the provision of a wife for Abraham, from whom the nation will descend (Genesis 24), then for Israel's deliverance from Egypt (Exodus 18), and finally for the promise of the building of the Temple (1 Kings 5). None of these events is a purely private concern; and it is clear that, even in these instances, the ascription of praise to God, while certainly on the lips of individuals, is born of Israel's corporate understanding of the nation's relationship with God. It is thus clear that the Benediction is already the focus of corporate prayer within the context of the people's worship.

The Benediction in Ephesians

There are examples of Benedictions in the literature at Qumran, and Paul himself writes one at the start of 2 Corinthians. The Benediction in Ephesians 1.3–14 is, according to Houlden (1977: 261) 'a distinct unit with a form and purpose of its own', and its context is probably that of baptism. Its form is closer to Old

Testament parallels than to those of the synagogue or Qumran, since it is in the third person – 'Blessed be God, who . . .' rather than 'Blessed be thou, who . . .'. He wonders whether it may be based on that in 2 Corinthians 1. He notes the centrality of Christ in its content and perceives its form as comprising three sections: vv. 3–6, vv. 7–12 and vv. 13–14.

Kirby locates the Benediction in Ephesians in the very precise context of the liturgical calendar in use at the time (1968: 145). He attempts to show how the lections for Pentecost were particularly appropriate for baptism, which he regards as the context for the Epistle to the Ephesians. Mitton (1976: 43) draws attention to the liturgical context of the Ephesian Benediction. He notes that it consists of one sentence, and that its elevated style is marked by a prominence of word doublings. He doubts Houlden's claim that it has 'its own life and history', and notes the degree to which it consists of phrases from Paul. He clearly regards Kirby's explanation as far too complex, and states that its style may be accounted for by the fact that it was intended for reading aloud. Mitton locates the origin of the Benediction in the worship of the Jewish home, particularly in the saying of grace at mealtimes. He agrees with Kirby that the worship of the synagogue and that of Qumran may have influenced the writer of the Epistle to the Ephesians to some extent, though he points out that this Benediction appears to be particularly dependent on 2 Corinthians 1.3, in that it has the same structure.

Whatever their particular understanding of the Ephesian Benediction, these various scholars are agreed that the context in this epistle is primarily liturgical. That is to say, the writer has in some way taken one central element of early Christian corporate praying and consciously based upon it a treatise, or homily, or meditation, upon a theological theme which he wishes to develop. The worship of the community has provided both the context and the literary form for reflection upon the action of God through Christ.

Some scholars have attempted to locate beneath the Ephesian Benediction the structure of an underlying early Christian hymn. The various attempts at reconstructions of these hymns, such as those by Schille (1953, 1957), Coutts (1956) and Fischer (1973), indicate the ingenuity of the various reconstructors, but remain unconvincing. This is mainly because the style of Ephesians 1 is consistent with the rest of the epistle, and the attempt to isolate underlying sources fails to convince. Moreover, such a passage as 5.14 would indicate that the writer of Ephesians makes it quite clear when he is quoting other material. It is more reasonable to conclude that there is no hymn underlying 1.3–14, but rather that this passage, along with the whole of the rest of the letter, constitutes a sustained piece of liturgically charged theological writing.

Kirby (1968: 136) analyses the structure of the Jewish Bene-diction as consisting of blessing, anamnesis and doxology. This is similar to the blessing in 1 Peter, but there it is followed im-mediately by a section of paraenesis, which in the case of Ephesians comes at the end of the letter. Ephesians is thus 'closer to the tradition'. Various other suggestions have been put forward for the analysis of the structure of the Benediction, including Lohmeyer (1926), Dahl (1951), Maurer (1951–2), Dibelius (1953), Masson (1953), Schille (1953, 1957) and Barth (1974).

An option which has the advantage of being rooted in the form rather than the content of the Benediction would note that whatever 'stanzas' are to be located are bounded not by the finite verbs, nor by verbal participles, nor by the word 'just as', but by the phrase 'to the praise of his glory'. This would give three stanzas of unequal length, certainly, but they would focus upon three factors of the writer's theological understanding, as it is expressed in the community's worship. These three factors are: the will of God, expressed primarily in election (vv. 3–6); the enactment of this will as the granting of redemption and enlightenment in Christ (vv. 7–12); and the experience of 'sealing' by the Spirit, by which these blessings are known (vv. 13–14). We shall look at each of these in turn.

The will of God

In 1.3–6 the writer blesses God for the election, or choice, of all believers 'in Christ' – 'just as he chose us in him before the foundation of the world' (1.4). Election is a fundamental Jewish idea, which can be traced back to the nation of Israel's sense of being God's chosen people. Rowley (1950) dismisses the view, put forward by Powis Smith (1928–9), that the Hebrew doctrine differed little from that of other religions in the ancient Near East, by referring to Deuteronomy 7.6ff., which roots the concept in God's love for the nation; it was not that Israel was better than any other. Moran (1992: 61) highlights the irony in the sense of chosenness: 'The Midrash says that God offered the covenant to everyone else before offering it to the Jews; the others thought it was a bad deal, the Jews did not ask.'

Rowley notes (1950: 19) that the election of Israel appears in some passages to be rooted in the time of the patriarchs (e.g. Isaiah 51.2, 41.8; Micah 7.20; Psalm 105.5–10, 43). In other passages it is located in the time of Moses (cf. Hosea 11.1; Jeremiah 2.2; Ezekiel 20.5). Rowley argues in favour of the patriarchal period and noted that this election has certain implications for Israel; in particular, it is election for service. Election is closely connected with the covenant, and Israel is to be God's servant. In Deutero-Isaiah (that is, chapters 40–55 of the Book of Isaiah, generally regarded as the work of a prophet later than Isaiah of Jerusalem of the eighth century BC), the emphasis is on mission to the world, in the sense that Israel's function is as the focus for God's saving will for the world. Election could be repudiated by the nation's sinful action, and was subject to God's judgment. However, his mercy guaranteed the constancy of his calling, and is retained in the idea of the remnant.

Rowley also refers (1950: 95ff.) to the election of individuals, such as Saul, David and other kings. The prophets Isaiah and Jeremiah are typical of prophets in general, who are reckoned to be subject to God's choice. The figure of the Servant in Deutero-Isaiah, in so far as he is an individual representing the nation, may perhaps be regarded as spanning both the individual and the corporate categories of divine election.

Finally, Rowley refers (1950: 121ff.) to a concept of election without covenant, with reference to the nations and their rulers whom God raises up to serve his particular purposes, such as Assyria and Cyrus of Persia.

However, when Rowley goes on to discuss 'the heirs of election' his understanding of the concept is insufficiently christological. He focuses on the church, and on Christians, but he fails to note the primary sense in which it is Christ who is the object of God's election. As far as the Epistle to the Ephesians is concerned, Christ is clearly the anointed one, though hardly in the same sense in which a prophet is anointed; the title is by now traditional and honorific, rather than to be regarded as referring to royal, prophetic or priestly offices. However, Christ is certainly, for the writer of Ephesians, the true nation of Israel, which consists of both Jew and Gentile; and the church is his body. In these senses the election of the people of God is involved in God's election of Christ. Hence the writer's frequent repetition of 'in Christ' or 'in him'.

There is an apparent distinction drawn by the writer in the use of 'we' and 'you' between Jewish and Gentile Christians in this passage. However, this does not become apparent until the intrusive use of 'in whom you also' in 1.13, following the use of 'who hoped before' in 1.12. There is therefore no emphatic distinction drawn between the two groups at the beginning of the Benediction, and this suggests that the difference between Jewish and Gentile Christians should not be pressed. All the believers are the recipients of the blessings contained in the Benediction; it is likely that the contrast which is introduced in Ephesians 1.13 is for the sake of the added emphasis which the writer wishes to give to his praise of God's grace. He is not concerned to talk of 'us' (Jews) and 'you' (Gentiles) in an exclusive manner, but rather of 'us' – all of us – and especially (all of) 'you' (Gentiles), in an inclusive way. To read the text thus is to take seriously its emphasis on unity.

The phrase 'before the foundation of the world' (1.4) is reminiscent of the Johannine 'high priestly' prayer in John 17.24, and it expresses again the idea of the election of the church as necessarily involved in the election of Christ. The Johannine passage understands Christ's death as for all the people, in that Jesus prays 'I do not pray for these alone, but also for those who will believe because of their word, that they all may be one, just as you, Father, are in me, and I in you.' According to John the Jewish leaders fear that the Romans will come and take away both their 'place', namely the Temple, and their nation (John 11.48). For the writer of Ephesians, the sacrifice of Christ brings about the establishment of the new Temple and the extension of the nation of Israel to embrace the Gentiles. The notion of Christ's sacrifice is continued with the sacrificial language in the expression 'that we should be holy and spotless before him'. This is also of interest in the light of the discussion of the marriage imagery of Ephesians 5.22–33 in chapter 7 below. The concept of the community being a new Temple adds further substance to the sacrificial imagery used here.

If the two words 'in love' at the end of 1.4 are intended to be taken with the preceding clause, they sound like an afterthought, though they express the writer's constant awareness of the bountiful grace of God in this work of salvation. However, they make more sense if they are taken as belonging to the participle which follows – 'having predestined'. This would remove the awkwardness of the phrase, as well as link the concept of love with that of 'sonship' (1.5), to which the believers are said to be destined, or marked out. This blessing is also 'through Jesus Christ', to whom the status of sonship applies in a primary sense. Sonship is also said to be 'to him', where the pronoun clearly refers to God; the sonship of the Gentiles along with Jews is thus is both in accordance with God's good pleasure – 'according to the good pleasure of his will' – and for his glory.

The first section of the Benediction therefore finishes with the phrase 'to the praise of the glory of his grace, which he has given us by grace in the Beloved' (1.6). This is the first of three such statements in the course of the Benediction, though not all three are identical. The constancy of 'to the praise of his glory' in each, with appropriate variation, adds to the liturgical atmosphere. The words added after this first occurrence focus, appropriately, upon God's grace, which is 'graciously given' to the believers 'in the Beloved'. This title is found only here in the New Testament, though it is also used as a title of Christ in the *Epistle of Barnabas* 3.6. Christ as the 'Son' is the primary object of God's love; and those who believe are also recipients of that love, because they constitute the Son's body.

Redemption and enlightenment in Christ

In 1.7–12 the writer blesses God for those blessings which might be regarded as more specifically 'christological'. In particular, he focuses upon redemption, forgiveness and the granting of the knowledge of God's will (1.7–9). This is the central section of the Benediction, and it embraces the primary focus of God's action. What was set out as his plan in 1,3–6 is here carried out, for the believers to experience. The *anakephalaiôsis* thus comes as the climax to the divine plan, and involves redemption, forgiveness and enlightenment. The twin concepts of redemption and forgiveness of sins in vv. 7–8 are derived as understandings of the cross from Pauline tradition.

Clearly, words like 'redemption' and 'forgiveness' (1.7) here are used as religious terms which would be familiar within the community's life. The meaning here may be either 'redemption' or 'deliverance', with a focus either upon the means or upon the experience of salvation. It is unnecessary to rule out either sense, in view of the liturgical context, where reference to both means and

experience would be appropriate. If the reference is to means, the
word implies the payment of something in order to secure redemption, and God is praised for giving his Son in payment. It is
not said to whom payment is made, and the analogy should not be
pressed so far as to demand an answer to this question, since the
liturgical context renders it inappropriate. The importance of the
readers' experience of redemption draws attention to the fact that
this is no mere theological abstraction; both writer and readers
know that they have been delivered by God in Christ from the
powers of evil, and it is nothing less than their knowledge of God
which assures them of this. The fact that it is theirs 'through his
blood' (1.7) again reinforces the notion of sacrifice present in the
whole passage.

The concept of redemption is thus closely linked with the
'forgiveness of sins' (1.7). Mitton (1976: 53) asserts that 'forgiveness' strictly means 'removal', so that the experience referred to is
actually one of the removal, not just of the effects, but also of the
presence of sin. However, he does not develop this point. It is, in
fact, quite likely that the noun is now so conventional in describing
this aspect of the benefits of Christ's sacrifice, that the etymology
of the word is of less value than its contextual use.

Certainly the sense of wonder is strong; the use both of the
expression 'according to the richness of his grace' (1.7) and of the
verb 'abounded' (1.8) indicates that the writer is convinced of the
great riches of the grace which the believers have been shown. Such
loftiness of expression, again, is appropriate for the liturgical
context. However, to it is added the idea that this redemption
involves also the imparting of knowledge (1.9). The blessing of the
granting of knowledge in vv. 9–12 is the immediate context in
which the verb 'to sum up' is used. This aspect of God's grace shown
in Christ's saving action centres on the sharing of the 'mystery' of
God's will. This 'mystery' – the secret which is now revealed – is the
'summing up' of all things, both in heaven and on earth. 'All
things' has therefore a clear reference to humanity, though the
whole creation is not to be ruled out. As the writer proceeds to
elaborate in the extended Thanksgiving, which takes up the next
chapter in the epistle, it involves both the reconciliation of God
with humanity, and the bringing together of Jew and Gentile in the
one body of Christ.

The 'summing up' is accomplished 'in Christ' (1.10), which
echoes Paul's own use of this latter term throughout the epistles,

though its meaning is more instrumental here than in, say, 1 Corinthians 1.2,5,30; Romans 8.1,2,39. The believers share the inheritance with Christ of all that he inherits. They also therefore share in this 'summing up', since this is the good pleasure of God, who is active in 'all things' in order to bring about the 'summing up' which he has willed – 'according to the good pleasure of him who accomplishes all things'.

The phrase 'to the praise of his glory' (1.12) here marks the end of the specifically 'christological' section. The participle 'hoped before' (1.12) and the following words 'in whom you also' together appear to make a distinction between those to whom the gospel was initially directed, namely the old nation of Israel, and those who may now believe, thanks to the preaching of the apostle Paul. This is, in many respects, a surprising distinction to make, in view of the writer's later concern for the oneness of the body of Christ. It is best understood therefore, as has been suggested above (see p. 47), as an emphasis for this particular point in the Benediction, rather than suggestive of any desire in the writer to make a thoroughgoing distinction between the two groups. Indeed, the absence of any thoroughgoing distinction is presupposed in the following two verses in praise of the Holy Spirit, with the reference to 'our' inheritance in v. 14. All the believers, whether Jew or Gentile, share the same inheritance, and this is spelled out in the latter half of the second chapter of the epistle.

Sealing in the Spirit

Ephesians 1.13–14 blesses God for the 'seal' of the Holy Spirit. In both Greek and Hebrew literature 'sealing' has to do with the identity and ownership of the thing sealed, as well as the authority and power of the one who seals. The metaphor of 'sealing' is found in Paul's own writing in 2 Corinthians 1.22 ('who has sealed us and given us the earnest of the Spirit'). The experience of the Spirit is therefore the sense of the believers' identity, their belonging to God through Christ, and the authority of Christ in their life. These are all known in baptism, which is common to all the believers and which takes place as a result of hearing and believing the gospel, the word of truth which is preached ('having heard the word of truth, the gospel of your salvation, in which you who believed . . .'). Here, as in 2 Corinthians, it is the 'first instalment' (1.14), the 'earnest', of the inheritance, to be received against final redemption, to which it looks forward. The Holy Spirit is the 'seal', given to the community and its members as the guarantee, or 'down payment' which looks forward to eventual possession. There is therefore an element of tension here between present experience and future hope.

The final use of the phrase 'to the praise of the glory' (1.14) simply centres upon God who has willed the consummation, who has made it possible in Christ, and who is known by his Spirit in the sealing of those who hear the gospel and respond. The writer is therefore praising the unity of the whole plan of God, brought to effect in Christ, and known by the church through the Spirit. It embraces both Jew and Gentile, and also (as is developed later in Ephesians 4–6) demands appropriate behaviour on the part of those who respond to it.

This analysis of the Benediction in sections according to the use of the phrase 'to the praise of the glory' indicates a threefold structure. It is significant to note that the atmosphere is liturgical; this lends weight to the earlier discussion of *lex orandi, lex credendi* in chapter 2, in so far as it indicates the extent to which the practice of praying in such triadic forms paved the way for the later development of trinitarian doctrine. The passage shows a high degree of liturgical colouring. Its language breathes the atmosphere of worship, and the refrain 'to the praise of the glory' is redolent of liturgical usage. For this reason, as well as because of the content of the Benediction, it is also eschatological, for what God planned before creation has now come to pass in Christ: the Gentiles are now also heirs of this ultimate act of God.

Chapter 4

Thanksgiving

After the Benediction in Ephesians 1.3–14, the epistle proceeds with a 'Thanksgiving', the title of which takes its name from the verb in 1.16, 'I do not cease to *give thanks* . . .', and it extends from 1.15 to the end of Ephesians 2. Thanksgiving was a significant element in ancient letters, including those of the apostle Paul. In Ephesians, a petitionary prayer precedes the main, teaching content of the Thanksgiving, which spells out the meaning of the 'summing up' of all things in Christ as Ephesians understands it.

Letters in the hellenistic world always began with a 'Thanksgiving', an expression of thanks to the gods for the health of the recipient, or for the news about him or her that the writer had received. Paul continued this convention, giving thanks for what he had heard about the well-being and discipleship of his readers. Indeed, the Thanksgivings in Paul's letters represent an important feature of his thought; namely that the idea of 'thanksgiving' was central to his theology, for it is used to introduce the main theological content of his letters (Schubert 1939). The most straightforward example of the Thanksgiving form is to be found in Philemon 4–5 ('I thank my God, always making mention of you in my prayers, having heard of your love and faith . . .'. This gives rise to a petition in v. 6 ('that the sharing of your faith may promote the knowledge of all the good that is ours in Christ').

The Thanksgivings share a common structure in that, in each case: (a) the verb 'give thanks' is employed in the first person singular or plural; (b) it is followed by the dative object 'to God'; and (c) there is always a definite addressee: 'The rhythmical interchange between the first and second persons is a structurally basic and characteristic element of the thanksgiving pattern' (Schubert 1939: 37).

This formal feature of Paul's letters did not escape the attention of his imitators. The Thanksgiving in Ephesians follows the basic pattern, but with some differences. It is introduced by the present participle 'giving thanks for you'; it is lengthy, in that it continues until the end of Ephesians 2; and it is interrupted by a petition, introduced by the words 'making mention . . . that', whereas most Thanksgivings state immediately some cause for the giving of thanks. This is a feature common to much epistolary literature in this period (cf. Philemon, Philippians, Colossians, 1 and 2 Thessalonians), but the change in emphasis is more abrupt here.

M. Barth (1974: 145ff.), who believes Ephesians to be by Paul, claims that it is typical of Paul to interrupt more general descriptions of God's relation to the church and the world with references to himself. Barth says that this is not a rhetorical device, but it expresses a high apostolic self-consciousness which has its roots in the function entrusted to the apostle by God. He refers to Romans 7.24–5 and Galatians 1.10–2.21, where the alleged digressions are made for particular theological purposes. It might be more reasonable to suggest that Ephesians copies it in these various contexts, in an attempt to create verisimilitude. Here, the petition is longer than in other letters, and it anticipates the content of the Thanksgiving to follow.

The participle 'having heard' is interesting (1.15). Barth sees it as evidence of 'the hearsay acquaintance between the writer and his addressees'. It makes more sense, however, to regard it as evidence that the letter was not originally to Ephesus; nor was it written by Paul; again, it is a pseudo-Pauline attempt at verisimilitude. It serves to highlight the question of the relationship between the author, the text and the reader. With the expression 'faith in the Lord Jesus' the epistle combines 'faith in' with 'faithfulness to' which is shared within any community in which Jesus is the Lord. The words 'the love which you have for all the saints' (1.15) are the subject of some textual confusion, with some texts omitting the phrase. Others have the words 'the love' in different positions in the clause. The confusion is probably to be explained by a scribal error in which scribes missed out words because of the similarity in the opening letters of words they are copying, in the mistaken repetition of a definite article, and various attempts by other scribes to remove the resulting confusion.

The expression 'I do not cease' (1.16) also occurs in the Thanksgiving in Colossians 1.9 (cf. Philemon 4; 1 Thessalonians

1.2; Colossians 1.3; Philippians 1.4; 1 Corinthians 1.4; 2 Thessalonians 1.3 and 2.13; also 1 Thessalonians 2.13 and 2.1–3; Romans
1.9–10; along with 1 Thessalonians 3.10; Romans 1.8. Thanksgiving
and petition mingle in all of these to some degree, though the
element of actual thanksgiving is not so distant as it is here.

The words 'remembering you in my prayers' are conventional in
letters of the period. Here the text takes the theme further, and
makes a specific petition, that 'the Father of glory' will grant the
readers 'the wisdom and insight that comes from knowing God'.
This is to lead to their knowledge of three things: (a) what is the
hope of their calling; (b) what are the riches of the glory of their
inheritance in the saints; and (c) the excessive greatness of his
power 'to us who believe'. Both the second and the third points
may be regarded as epexegetical of the first, according to Schlier
(1963), but the repetition of 'what is' seems to indicate otherwise,
as does the structure of the section 1.19–22, as we shall see.

For Ephesians, an understanding of Christ gives rise to an
understanding of the church. The divine power at work in believers
is that which was at work in the resurrection of Christ (1.20); the
saints' inheritance (1.21) is to share in the dominion of Christ 'in
the heavenlies' over the powers; and the hope to which they are
called is, above all, membership of the church (1.22–3). The
structure of 1.19–23 is therefore chiastic: the resurrection of Christ
corresponds with the power which is at work in believers; the
inheritance is a share in the dominion of Christ; and the hope is
grounded in the life, the growth and the consummation of the
church. Power, inheritance and hope have, all three, a present as
well as a future reference, since what has happened looks forward
to what is yet to be, and the exalted style indicates the setting of all
this in the church's worship.

The chiastic structure of the petition underlines the liturgical
context in which the epistle is set. The petition is addressed to God,
and the subject of its verbs is God. It is God who grants the spirit
of wisdom and understanding; the great power at work in the
believers, which is the same power which was at work in the
resurrection of Christ, is God's; and it is God who has subjected
all things to Christ by making him head of – that is, source for –
the church.

The appointment of Christ to headship for the church recalls the
major christological point made in the Benediction; that the
ultimate plan of God is to 'sum up' all things in him, even though

the reasons for the giving of thanks are not set out in detail until Ephesians 2. The concept of 'summing up' is thus both the focus of the Benediction and the climax of the petition. It is therefore appropriate that it should be the subject of further development in the passage which follows. The reason for the giving of thanks is now spelt out in 2.1ff., and the two sections 2.1–10 and 2.11–22 are closely parallel in form.

THE TWO REALMS

After the opening in 1.15–23 the reasons for the Thanksgiving are set out in 2.1–22. The climax of the petition is what is said about Christ's headship in 1.22. We noted that the statement in 1.10, concerning the 'summing up' of all things by means of Christ, is the climax of the Benediction, in that it makes clear the ultimate purpose of God. The whole of Ephesians 2 spells out the content of this 'summing up', and develops it in terms of 'things in heaven' and 'things on earth'. The two realms are seen to belong together as the spheres over which God reigns through the resurrection and exaltation of Christ.

That the two sections belong together is further evidenced by the parallel structure of their content, in that both in turn deal with: (a) the former state of both Gentiles and Jews; (b) the nature of the saving act of God; and (c) the sense in which salvation is both already known and also yet to be known in its effects within the realms in which it is effected. We shall take a look at these three elements of the structure in each half of the Thanksgiving.

In the heavenlies

The passage 2.1–10 divides naturally into three parts: (a) verses 1–3, in which the writer describes the previous state of the Gentiles; (b) verses 4–6, in which the writer describes how salvation has been achieved; and (c) verses 7–10, in which the blessings of the present state are spelled out.

The characterization of the Gentiles' former state (2.1–3)

In the realm of 'the heavenlies' the former state of believers is characterized by an enmity between humanity and God which is to be defeated through God's action. The writer makes it clear that this state was not peculiar to Gentiles, but was shared also by Jews (2.3). There are seven characteristics of the former life, and they all involve submission to the control of hostile forces:

1 death in trespasses and sins (2.1, repeated in 2.5);
2 subjection to the powers (2.2);
3 living among the sons of disobedience (2.2);
4 living in the lusts of the flesh (2.3);
5 fulfilling the desires of flesh and mind (2.3);
6 being children of wrath (2.3);
7 leading an existence undifferentiated from that of others (2.3).

Some examination is therefore required of this terminology.

The widespread debate concerning the cosmological language of Ephesians was particularly focused by the 'history of religions' school, who suggested that the language of cosmological specu-lation in this section derived from contemporary religions such as Gnosticism and Mithraism, as well as Judaism. Death is a sign of sin in Ephesians – as it was for Paul (cf. Romans 5; 1 Corinthians 15) – and it also involves a kind of subjection to hostile spiritual powers. These powers are those to be found inhabiting the region above the earth. However, there are antecedents within Jewish tradition for this line of thinking. Barth (1974: 102), noting that the Hebrew word for heaven is the plural noun *shemayim*, points out that this does not imply that all Hebrew writers had a uniform understand-ing of a plurality of heavens. Paul speaks of a hierarchy of heavens in 2 Corinthians 12.2; a topography of heaven is provided in 1 Enoch 20–36; and in 2 Enoch 8–10 paradise and hell are found to be in the same sphere. However, another possible background area for the language of Ephesians 2 is that which later developed into Gnosticism; the thirty 'aeons' express and constitute the pleroma of divine beings. In the references also to 'archons', there may be a hint of the idea of planets determining fate with an iron grip.

Carr (1981) argues very strongly in favour of a predominantly Jewish interpretation of the angelic world of Ephesians and rejects any idea that hellenistic cosmology has influenced the writer (and he takes this to be Paul) in his elaboration of the former state of the Gentiles in Ephesians 2. Carr insists that the distinction being made here is purely that between two ages of history. Following on from this, he insists, quoting 2 Enoch 29.4 and Job 1.7, upon an understanding of the word translated 'air' in 2.2 which is one not of locality, but of universality. His consequent translation of the passage in Ephesians 2 runs as follows:

> You were dead in your trespasses and sins. Once upon a time you lived your life in such sins according to the ways of the old age, the age of this world, according to the devil, the prince whose power is universal and inescapable, according to that spirit which is even now at work in the apostates and moral failures among us.
>
> (1981: 103)

Carr's insistence upon an *exclusively* Jewish background fails to take into account the extent to which religious and philosophical ideas crossed cultural boundaries. He fails to notice that, even though the background to the thought in Ephesians 2 (and 6.10ff.) cannot be regarded as 'Gnostic' in the proper, second-century sense of the term, it is sufficiently distinctive in its emphases to allow of the possibility that it marked a stage along the way towards that later development, and may well have been one of the factors which made possible the subsequent establishment of Gnostic ideas on a broader scale. His thesis concludes with the unconvincing contention:

> Far from being a fundamental part of the background and proclamation of the Christian message, the notion of the mighty forces of evil ranged against man was not part of the earliest Christian understanding of the world and the gospel. There is nothing in the Pauline writings that refers to a battle between Christ and hostile forces. Indeed, it is also noticeable that there is no conflict directly between Christ and Satan.
>
> (1981: 176–7)

Lincoln's study (1981) provides a broader understanding of the context of thought in which this letter may have been written (and the author confesses in a footnote that he changed his mind about the question of Pauline authorship in the period between the writing of the thesis and its preparation for publication as a book). He locates the epistle very firmly in the worship of the early Christian community and states that 'an examination of "in the heavenlies . . ." indicates that it is used as a formula which retains the same meaning throughout and that the meaning which is most appropriate to all five contexts is a local one' (1981: 14).

Lincoln acknowledges that the later Gnostic writings made much of Paul but suggests that there was in the Jewish background to Paul's thought a sufficiently developed idea of the righteous entering into eschatological dominion and life and sitting on heavenly thrones (cf. Daniel 7.22,27; Wisdom of Solomon 3.8; 5.15,16; 1 Enoch 108.12; Apocalypse of Elijah 37.3,4; Testament of Job 33.3–5; Revelation 3.21; Ascension of Isaiah 9.18). The Qumran documents also speak of redemption of the soul 'from the Pit and from the Hell of Abaddon. Thou hast raised me up to everlasting height. Thou hast cleansed a perverse spirit of great sin that it may enter into community with the congregation of the Sons of Heaven' (1QH 3.19–22). Thus the community believed itself to be entering into the heavenly sanctuary in their own worship, since it regarded itself as the eschatological temple (1QS 8.4ff.; 9.3ff.; cf. Vermes 1962: 158, 85ff.).

What is noteworthy about Ephesians is the view that 'the heavenlies' have space not only for Christ and believers, but also for the hostile powers. This may be explained upon the basis of an understanding of the cosmos which sees the heavens as the dwelling place of the whole 'spirit' world. Such a view is to be found in the Old Testament in Job 1.6 and Daniel 10.13,21; and in apocalyptic thought in such passages as 2 Maccabees 5.2; 1 Enoch 61.10; 90.21,24. It also occurs in Philo (*De Spec. Leg.* I.66, *De Plant.* 14, *De Gig.* 6f.). Hence the significance of the demonstration to the powers in the heavenly realm of the victory of God in Ephesians 3.10, and hence also the significance of the final struggle waged in Ephesians 6.10ff. in the heavenly realm itself.

Ephesians expresses the contrast between the new creation and the old by bringing together a number of religious and philosophical speculative currents in order to develop an understanding of the position of both Jews and Gentiles in a hostile world. Clearly, the Gentiles before their salvation were under the control of the hostile powers. The fact that these powers are present to God in the heavenly realm might even be said to add to the urgency of God's concern for their defeat, for it is as if God's authority and honour within his own realm is at stake. Clearly, however, this honour is not at variance with a gracious love for the creation.

The act of saving (2.4–6)

God, consequently, has considerable interest in the obtaining of salvation for all. That this is nevertheless a result of the riches of his mercy is not in doubt; indeed, it adds to the degree to which he invests something of himself in the plan of salvation.

The Gentiles' former state is reversed by the gracious intervening activity of God. This is 'through his great love with which he loved us' (2.4), which is a typical Ephesian pleonasm. God is the subject of the verbs throughout this passage, and it is God whose actions, through the agency of Christ, bring about the Gentiles' salvation. Yet, clearly, for the writer of Ephesians as for the apostle Paul, God is perceived to act in Christ, making him the focus of the divine saving activity. This is most clearly brought out in the verbs which carry the prefix *sun-*, which means 'together', for it is Christ who is the primary object of the action of the verbs; the believers are included along with him in being made alive together, in being raised together and in being made to sit together with Christ 'in the heavenlies'.

Much discussion has taken place over the time at which the action of God in 'giving life' took place ('made us alive together', 2.5). Abbott (1897: 47) reports that Meyer, 'having understood "dead" to refer to future, eternal death, of course understands "he has quickened us together" as referring to the eternal life which begins at the resurrection.' The use of an aorist to express a future meaning is said to be paralleled in a passage of Homer (*Iliad* IV. 160–2) as well as in John 15.6. However, as Abbott points out, '"dead" includes present, spiritual death, and that indeed as its primary notion ... Accordingly, the vivification includes in it our share in the resurrection and exaltation of Christ.' Abbott draws attention to the fact that, in Ephesians 1.20–1, the writer has pointed to the resurrection and exaltation of Christ as 'an exhibition of divine power; here he declares that by virtue of our union with him as members with the head, we participate in the same'.

Indeed, the implication of this passage is the significant assertion that the resurrection of Christ has effected not only his being raised from the dead, but inevitably also that of believers, who are incorporate in him by baptism. Thus the liturgical context of the letter, especially if related specifically to the liturgy of baptism, makes the connection between the baptismal rite and the resurrection of Christ which is common to early baptismal texts. What is emphasized here, however, is the relationship established by God between Christ and the believer, namely, one of essential unity. The 'together' verbs have the effect of emphasizing the extent to which the believers are the object of the same divine action as Christ himself at his resurrection. What is more, the resurrection, which involved both the giving of life and the action of raising from the dead, was, at the same time, the moment of the glorification of Christ in the heavenly realm.

Since this heavenly realm is the realm in which the spiritual world has its being, and not necessarily that in which God dwells to the exclusion of hostile powers, it is worth noting that the dwelling place of the church is consequently precisely the place where the spiritual powers are gathered, and where the church may be seen by them as the glorious creation of God. Thus 'he has shown' in Ephesians 2.7 does not mean simply 'exhibit in fact or act' as Abbott says but 'make known' as Schlier (1963: 112–13) and Houlden (1977: 28) interpret it.

As Abbott points out, 'we are so accustomed to use the word "grace" in a technical religious sense, that we are prone to forget the simple meaning which it so often has, "undeserved bounty", "free gift"' (1897: 49) He refers to Romans 3.24 ('his gift of grace'), and to Romans 11.5 ('according to the good pleasure of his grace'), as well as Ephesians 2.5. It is this grace that is the divine motive in the act of salvation. The reminder in parentheses in Ephesians 2.5 is taken up again in v. 8. The 'death' which prevailed over the Gentiles in their former state ('dead in trespasses and sins', 2.1) rendered them incapable of any action to save themselves, thus God's action was essential if anything was to be done for their salvation at all.

What is striking about this passage in Ephesians is the use of the verb 'save' (2.5,8) where, we might suppose, Paul himself would have employed 'justify'. This change in terminology in the Pauline imitator is perhaps both because the language of justification is no longer intelligible, and it would not be appropriate to this context, since the discussion does not centre on the validity or otherwise of the Torah, the Jewish Law, in its effect upon humanity's standing before God. Moreover, the language of justification belongs specifically to the life and experience of Paul himself, and possibly to a polemical context in the setting of his own apostolic ministry (cf. Minear 1971). This would be a further reason why the writer of Ephesians may wish to avoid it in the later, more eirenical setting of this epistle.

The results of divine salvation (2.7–10)

The Gentiles' state is altered by God's gracious act of salvation in Christ. In the context of 'the heavenlies', the writer expresses the view that salvation is accomplished in order (a) to make known God's grace 'in the coming ages'; and (b) to bring about results in the realm of the church's moral experience. We shall look at each of these in turn.

The interpretation of 'in the coming ages' is a far from straightforward matter. First, the word 'in' might alternatively mean 'among'. Second, the word 'coming' might alternatively mean 'present' or 'coming upon' in the sense of 'attacking'. Third, the word 'ages' might alternatively mean 'aeons' in the technical sense of the 'principalities and powers' as they were later understood in Gnostic systems.

In Ephesians, the realm where God dwells is also the realm of the hostile powers, so 'among' would make good sense here. Ephesians shows very little interest in 'the world to come', and speaks consistently in terms of an eschatology which is 'realized' in the present experience of the Christian community. Lindemann (1975) understands the concept of time in Ephesians to have been replaced by that of space; the text makes use of temporal language, which would be part of the general Pauline and early Christian background, in order to elaborate a more self-consciously spatial conception of earthly and spiritual realities. There are difficulties with a wholesale acceptance of Lindemann's thesis, but it is possible here that this passage is an early example of the word *aeon* being used for the powers presided over by the 'prince of the power of the air' (2.2). The tendency for liturgical language to allow of several layers of meaning makes this possible, as does the language of Ephesians 6.10ff., where the battle between the church and evil powers is still being waged. The 'ages to come' are thus to be seen as the arena against which the Christian community will have to wage its struggle for the truth of the gospel. In this way the unceasing nature of the struggle is asserted.

The expression 'for we are his creation' – the Greek word is *poiema*, which comes from the verb 'to make' – is clearly a statement about the nature of God's creative activity as much as about the church's being. God's grace is known to the church in its experience. This is true of its experience of worship, especially of baptism, but also of its continuing life, which is addressed in chapters 4–6 of Ephesians.

The word group 'make' is associated, in both secular and biblical Greek, with the divine creation. Zeus is regarded as the creator of all things, including heaven and the gods, and Plato uses this verb to refer to creation by the chief deity (Kittel and Friedrich: TDNT VI, 458–84). The Septuagint uses the word for creation (Genesis 1.1,27; Proverbs 14.31) and for God's dealings in history (Ecclesiastes 1.14; Numbers 14.35; Ezekiel 5.10; Exodus 13.8, 15.11; Deuteronomy 11.3). Romans 1.20 has the only other New Testament occurrence of the noun *poiema* (in the plural), 'the things that are made'. New Testament writers do, however, add a further area of meaning to the verb, namely that of the specifically eschatological acts of God (cf., for example, Matthew 18.35; Luke 1.51, 18.7–8; Jude 15; Revelation 21.5).

The use of *poiema* in this verse, then, accords with an understanding of a new act of God (and the position of 'his' indicates emphasis upon *God's* creation) in the resurrection of Christ from the dead, in which those who are incorporate in him are also raised and exalted, and, further, constitute a new creation by God (cf. at Qumran, 1QH 1.21; 3.23; 4.29; 11.3; 12.26,32; 18.12,25,31). There is an obvious link with statements of Paul in Galatians 6.15 and 2 Corinthians 5.17, as well as Colossians 3.10 and Ephesians 4.24 (and the immediately subsequent use of 'create'). Such statements clearly reflect a baptismal background, as does the exhortation to good works which follows. The divine initiative, however, extends also to these good works, 'which God has foreordained, that we should walk in them'. The expression used in Romans 9.23 for the predestination of Israel is applied here to the area of life for which the believer might normally expect to have to take responsibility. Such good works thus share in the election mentioned in Ephesians 1.4–5.

In stating that the church is God's creation 'for good works, that we should walk in them' (2.10), Ephesians indicates that the saving act of God is made known in the realm of behaviour. The theme of 'walking' is taken up again in 4.1 ('walk worthy'), 4.17 ('walk not as the Gentiles'), 5.1 ('walk in love'), 5.7 ('walk in light'), 5.15 ('walk wisely'), in the specifically ethical section of the letter.

On earth

The second section of Ephesians 2 – verses 11–22 – spells out the 'earthly' dimension of God's 'summing up' of all things in Christ.

Like the first half of the chapter, it also divides naturally into three parts: (a) verses 11–13, in which the writer describes the previous state of the Gentiles; (b) verses 14–16 (possibly 17), in which he shows how salvation, understood as reconciliation, has been achieved; and (c) verses 17 (possibly 18)–22, in which their present state is spelled out.

It is possible that such expressions as 'remember . . . formerly' in 2.11 and 'at that time' in 2.12 draw attention to something which the readers must already know. Abbott (1897: 55) takes the verb 'remember' at face value, as do most other commentators. Houlden, however, raises the possibility that the emphasis on 'remembering' in this context may be a liturgical device simply meaning 'because' (in view of the absence of 'because'). He does nevertheless tend towards the view that it is a genuine reminder of something in danger of being forgotten (1977: 288). It is more likely, however, that these phrases are rhetorical, designed to prepare the way for a set of new ideas. This can hardly be a genuine call to remembrance if the letter is not an authentic letter of Paul's, and the device must be part of the pseudepigraphical framework. The admonition 'call to mind' is more than a reminder to them of their theological inheritance; it also draws their attention to the role of the apostle, whose task was the evangelization of the Gentiles. This emphasis will be developed in Ephesians 3.

The former state (2.11–13)

In the first half of the chapter, the previous state was characterized by subjection to inimical spiritual forces; in this second half, the parallel characteristic is alienation from the people of God. This meant that the readers, who are here characterized as the 'uncircumcision' (2.11), according to the view of the 'circumcised', were 'separated from Christ' (2.12), though, as the text makes clear, the distinction between circumcision and uncircumcision is no longer valid. Barth (1974: 256) understands the reference to 'Christ' here as a statement of belief in the pre-existence of the Messiah in Israel. However, it is more likely that it is an arresting assertion of the Gentiles' alienation, which is expounded in the phrases which follow. This conveys the idea of their separation from that total entity, Israel, in which alone the very concept of a 'Messiah' could have any meaning.

Nevertheless, the Gentiles were 'alienated from the polity of

Israel' (2.12). The word *politeia* could mean 'citizenship', as, for example, in Acts 22.28, 'I bought this citizenship for a great sum of money', but it seems more likely here to mean 'commonwealth', or 'community', or even 'ethos'; that which was determined by Israel's awareness of the presence among them of the 'covenants of promise'. To be strangers to that heritage meant that they 'had no hope and were without God in the world' (2.12), that is, they suffered a thorough-going, hopeless and cosmic alienation.

The act of saving (2.14–16)

In this central section of the second half of Ephesians 2, which deals with the act of salvation which has been accomplished by God, the focus is upon the person of Christ, rather than upon God, though it is clearly God who is perceived to be active in and through him (cf. the impersonal passive verb 'have been brought near'). In the context of 'the heavenlies', God, who is rich in mercy, has, by his great love, given life to, raised up and set the Gentile believers 'in the heavenlies', in order to display his grace to the heavenly powers (2.5–7). In the context of the history of the people of God 'on earth', Christ, by his blood, has brought near those who were far off. In Deutero-Isaiah, where the allusion originates, the reference was to the reconciliation of those people of Israel who were suffering exile as opposed to the remnant of Israel which had been left in Jerusalem. Here the focus is upon those who were formerly alienated altogether from God, who have now been incorporated into the polity of Israel.

The emphasis is not so much on a doctrine of atonement here, though, if there is one, it is clearly one of 'slaying the enmity', which must be seen as akin to defeat of the powers of evil (Aulén 1975). Rather, the writer is using imagery from the area of sacrifice, which was more or less common coin among Christian understandings of the death of Christ, to assert also the prior oneness of those, both Jew and Gentile, who are incorporate in Christ, who was the one sacrificial offering. When the writer says, 'for he is our peace' (2.14), he is asserting something which is common to the religious understanding of the readers. They know that the sacrifice effected access. If, therefore, one sacrificial offering was made (that is, if one body was offered, in which they all, both Jew and Gentile, were aware of participation by baptism), then Jew and Gentile must be one. Thus enmity was destroyed between them, the law was annulled, and *one* new 'man' was raised after the offering had been made. The barrier was abolished – and it was also seen to be abolished (2.14–16).

A crucial element in this passage, particularly for the interpretation offered in this *Reading*, is the expression 'the middle wall of partition' in Ephesians 2.14. Abbott (1897: 61), who considered the letter authentically Pauline, saw this 'middle wall of partition' as a reference to the dividing fence between the Court of the Gentiles and the Court of Israel in the Temple, and says that Paul is using it as an image for the hostility between Jew and Gentile (cf. the story in Acts 21.26 concerning Paul's taking Gentile converts into the Temple for their purification.) Indeed, there would appear to be very good reasons for accepting this as a reference to the wall in the Temple, and perceiving it as all the more significant, since Paul is not the author; the events of AD 70, and the destruction of the Temple in particular, have inspired the writer of Ephesians to see a theological connection between the death of Christ and what happened historically to the Temple. Paul's preaching of the gospel had already made clear that the cross brought about the salvation of the Gentiles. The writer to the Ephesians saw the breaking down of this 'dividing wall' as a vindication of what Paul preached. It demonstrated the validity of the apostle's understanding of the cross.

Barth seems to see the force of this possibility (1974: 263–4; 282–91), yet, as it would appear, since he is concerned to maintain Pauline authorship, he argues that this cannot be so, since the expression found in Josephus and Philo for this barrier – 'stone fence' – is not the one used in this passage. However, this expression can hardly be regarded as a technical term. The writer of Ephesians, though starting with that image, has no desire to be bound by it. Indeed, there are other allusions present: the Rabbinic idea of the fence around the law (did such an idea give rise to the fence in the Temple – or the other way round?), and the Septuagint version of Psalm 80.12, where the breaking down of the walls precedes the prayer for the hand of God to be 'upon the man of thy right hand, the son of man whom thou has made strong for thyself'. Houlden (1977: 290–1) also sees a reference to the concept of a wall which divides the spheres of heaven and earth, which is present in speculative Judaism of the period (1 Enoch 14.9) and developed in later Gnostic thought. This idea may not be entirely absent, but the division here is clearly upon the earth;

the wall divides Gentiles from Jews, not, in this passage, either of them from God.

The effect of the sacrifice is not only that access is established by the Spirit to the Father, but also that a new creation is brought into being, namely the church, which is the visible sign of unity between Jew and Gentile. It is designated the new 'man', which had its origin in the one man, Christ, who was offered on the cross. He embodied both Jew and Gentile in his sacrifice and brought about the inclusion of the Gentiles into the chosen people of God, reversing their former disadvantages and bringing to them the full privileges of membership of Israel's 'polity', which is the household of God.

The image then changes from that of the household to that of a building, which in turn becomes a temple, the dwelling place of God by the Spirit. A move is thus made from an understanding of the body of Christ as a sacrifice, to an understanding of it as the new community and the new Temple. The central concepts of his argument are thus brought together. Christ is the 'sacrifice' – normally offered in the Temple – which brings into being the community of Jew and Gentile which is the new and true Temple of God.

The results of divine salvation (2.17–22)

The writer's concern to elaborate the purpose of the salvation accomplished by God is treated in this second half of Ephesians 2 by a series of images. Whereas, in the first half of the chapter, the focus was upon making known the power of God to the heavenly powers, in this second half the writer hints at certain moral implications of God's gracious activity. The specific elaboration of this is the subject of the writer's exhortation which begins in 3.1, but which is interrupted for his praise of the apostle, and is therefore taken up again in 4.1 and carried through to the end of the epistle. In Ephesians 2 the writer contents himself with setting up the images which will introduce the concept of moral and spiritual growth in the church, which is determinative for the ethical material to follow later in the epistle.

The first image was that of the 'one new man' (2.15). Christ had been the sacrificial offering which made possible the unity between Jew and Gentile, and Christ is the one body in which this unity is now experienced. There may be an allusion here to the 'man' of Psalm 80.17, but the clearer reference is to Paul's concept of the

Second Adam, elaborated in 1 Corinthians 15.21ff., Philippians 2.6, Romans 5.12ff. and Colossians 3.10f. In so far as Adam was the first created man in the biblical story, this represents a further use of 'creation' language to refer to the saving act.

The second image is that of a household, the 'household of God' (2.19), within which there are no strangers or foreigners, since all are 'members'. Paul refers (Galatians 6.10) to the 'household of faith', and 1 Timothy 5.8 speaks of a man's duty to provide for his household. Here, the household is God's (cf. Moses's house in Hebrews 3.2 as an analogy for Christ's faithfulness 'as a son' in God's house, and the following statement, 'whose household we are'.) However, the reference is more concrete, for Ephesians proceeds to speak of the 'foundation' being the 'holy apostles and prophets', with 'Jesus Christ being the chief corner-stone' (2.20).

The idea of the community of God's people as the temple in which God dwells is familiar from the writings of the Essene community at Qumran, though here its cosmic significance is enlarged by the reference to the 'chief corner-stone' in Ephesians 2.20. Lincoln sees this (1981: 153) as a reference to 'the final stone of the building which was probably set over the gate'. McKelvey (1969: 203f.) argues, on the basis of one strand of Jewish tradition, that the cornerstone represents the underworld. Lincoln rightly points out, however, that this cannot be the case in Ephesians, since, as has been shown, the world of spirits is understood very differently. The underworld plays no part in Ephesians, and the Temple imagery here has not only eschatological, but also cosmic, significance.

This gives way to the third image, which is that of the building which grows into a holy temple. One striking feature of this passage is the significance of the work of the Spirit in these images of unity and growth. Ephesians 2.11–22 develops an understanding of the final act of God which is parallel to that in 2.1–10. Here the concern is with salvation as it is experienced on earth, whereas the first half of the chapter dealt with how it is experienced in the realm of spiritual realities.

In other words, the text is developing what was said in 1.10; God's plan is the 'summing up' of all things in Christ; this is effected in the two realms of God's creation, in the heavenlies and on earth. Attention has already been drawn to the fact that the statement concerning the 'summing up' occurs in the Benediction of Ephesians 1, that is, in the context of the church's worship, and several scholars have pointed out the likely baptismal origin for this passage. The Benediction is followed by a Thanksgiving, the form of which, as we have also indicated, is taken from the genuine letters of Paul. These are best designated 'liturgical letters', for they are particularly designed to be read in the context of the church's worship.

'TO SUM UP ALL THINGS IN CHRIST'

Prayers follow the Thanksgiving and are also to be found at the end of Ephesians 3 and Ephesians 6. The prayer in 1.17ff. is that the readers will perceive the end to which they are destined; in 3.14ff. it is that they will be empowered by the Spirit; in 6.18ff. it is that their prayers will perpetuate the apostle's ministry. Ephesians is concerned with the spiritual development of its readers. The whole tone of the letter underlines that this is a conscious piece of religious writing, in that it gives expression to a particular understanding of events, and seeks to enlarge the readers' sense of blessing and thanksgiving for God's saving acts. Ephesians takes seriously the moral implications of this, and these are worked out at greater length and in greater detail in the ethical section of the letter which begins at 4.1.

The Thanksgiving in Ephesians constitutes by far the longest section in the epistle – from 1.15 to 2.22 – and it expounds the statement in 1.10 that God's plan is 'to sum up all things in Christ'. This 'summing up' is not just the unity of human races, but the real involvement of God in human affairs encompassing also redemption, forgiveness and the creation of a new humanity. 'Summing up' in Ephesians involves two intersecting planes of meaning – the relationship between God and humanity, and the relationship between the races of humanity on earth.

In the context of the heavenly realm this 'summing up' involves an exercise of authority over the powers, in that they are obliged to note the saving activity of God. It also involves the uniting of humanity with God, and the verbs with the prefix *sun-* indicate the intrinsic oneness implied between Christ and the church. It also involves the renewal of humanity, which, as the church, is God's new creation and is destined to carry out the good works for which it was created. In the context of earth, 'summing up' involves a similar triad of divine activity: it is the act of uniting Jew and Gentile; it is the renewing of the creation as one 'new man'; and it is the power of God, perceived by believing Jews and Gentiles, in the reconciling action of Christ and in the work of the Spirit, who makes possible the moral development which is set out in the second half of the epistle.

In the light of this study of the theological content of the two halves of Ephesians 2, it is interesting to note that the lexical study of the 'summing up' word group yielded the very same area of meanings. As was noted in the word study, the verb may indeed be used of the areas of bringing to a conclusion, which fits the eschatological context of salvation; of uniting, which is linked here to the bringing together of Jew and Gentile in one body; and of renewing, which is appropriate for the development of an Adamic christology, and which is worked out more fully later. This would seem to be significant corroboration of the view that the writer deliberately chose this ambiguous word – 'to sum up' – from the context of rhetoric, to cover the areas of meaning he had in mind.

Chapter 5

The worthy walk

The fourth chapter of Ephesians begins the specifically 'persuasive' part of the epistle; what follows is what the readers are supposed to *do* in the light of the teaching they have received in the praise of God in Ephesians 1–2 and the memorial to Paul in chapter 3. This 'ethical' section (4.1–6.9) urges them to live a life appropriate for the community which is the object of the saving activity of God described in the Thanksgiving. The call is to 'walk', and the analogy is drawn from the general image in Jewish writing – *halakah* – for appropriate behaviour in the light of God's grace shown in the covenant with his people.

Writers in the Hebrew tradition – and this would include Paul and his imitators – raised no problem over the philosophical distinction between 'fact' and 'value' which we know in the West; philosophers now discuss whether appeals concerning behaviour can be made upon the basis of certain facts. The assumption Jewish writers made is that children of the covenant act as children of the covenant. Life was – and is – essentially moral for the Jews, because they saw – and see – themselves as bound by covenant to a God who first acted morally in delivering them from slavery in Egypt. He consequently demanded a response which mirrored his own action. Unlike Greek moral thought, Hebrew ethics saw no polarity between what is true and what is demanded: to narrate is to require. Neither was it appropriate to enquire into the validity of moral statements in the context of a God who demands obedience; God was not known in his essence, but in his actions, and his actions were plain from the narrative of the community. The possibility of his 'non-existence' therefore did not arise: he was (because he acted) he is (because he continues to act) and he is to come (not, 'he will be', for essence is not the issue) – for he will do something.

Paul's own letters comprised both proclamation and demand (Furnish 1968). For any Christian writer, especially one writing in the name of Paul, it would be unthinkable that 'doctrinal' teaching could be given in isolation from ethical instruction. The ethical section in Ephesians is dependent upon that in the letter to the Colossians, and it expands upon, or qualifies, it in several ways: first, in its emphasis on unity; second, in the image of walking (with its connotations of the relationship between movement and growth); third, in its use of catalogues and household codes; fourth, in the marriage imagery – the longest subject dealt with; and finally, to an extent, by the image of the armour of God – though this breaks out from the confines of mere ethical instruction.

The question has been raised as to why there is so much ethical material in Ephesians – amounting to half the document. Fischer (1973: 172) argues that the situation in which the epistle was written demanded it. The young Christians to whom Ephesians was addressed were in danger of breaking loose from their Pauline moorings. By appealing to forms of exhortation which link a Jewish ethos with Christian baptismal traditions, the text recalls them to the basics of their faith. However, the ethical section as a whole is about as long as the doxology and the memorial together, so the whole epistle retains a certain structural balance between teaching and instruction, which accords with Furnish's analysis of the Pauline ethic (1968: 224–7). This provides further evidence that the writer was a faithful continuator of the tradition he inherited.

Ephesians 4.1–16 marks the transition to direct instruction of behaviour after the Benediction, Thanksgiving, petition and memorial of Paul in Ephesians 1–3. The passage outlines the appropriate lifestyle of those who sound the praises of God. These people are reconciled to God and are incorporate together in the one body of Christ. They are part of the body which comprises both Jew and Gentile, brought into being by the death of Christ. This gospel was preached by the apostle Paul, and has now been vindicated triumphantly in the passing of God's historical verdict on the city of Jerusalem. To a greater extent than in any of Paul's own letters, Ephesians 4–6 is a structured piece of moral exhortation. Ephesians sets the context, the tone and the goal of the church's moral existence by making a connection between praise, memorial and exhortation. The whole exhortatory passage ends with the image of the armour of God in Ephesians 6.10ff., which constitutes also the climax and conclusion to the whole epistle.

The most natural division of the material is suggested by the occurrence of the verb 'to walk'. The word is used in the general sense of 'conduct one's life', as it is in Rabbinic thought, and it also echoes the language of earlier parts of the letter. In 2.2 the writer refers to the readers' former 'manner of life' among the Gentiles, and in 2.10 he contrasts this with the good works in which they are now fore-ordained to 'walk'.

In the ethical section of the epistle there are five exhortations to 'walk', namely: worthy of their calling (4.1); not like the Gentiles (4.17); in love (5.2); as children of light (5.8); and wisely, redeeming the time (5.15). For ease of handling these themes, we shall look at the first in this chapter, the second, third and fourth in chapter 6, and the fifth in chapter 7.

The readers are urged to 'walk worthily' of the calling they have received. They are destined to share a part in the final 'summing up' of all things in Christ; they must therefore conduct their lives in a way which accords with the awe-inspiring vocation both to know and to foster unity. The intrinsic oneness at the root of the believing community is elaborated in 4.1–6; it is amplified by a quotation from Psalm 68 and a 'midrashic commentary' on it in Ephesians 4.7–10. 'Midrash' is a term normally used for the exegesis of scripture by Jewish Rabbis; it aims both at providing lessons in how the Torah – or 'Law' – is to be observed, and at enabling understanding of scriptures which are otherwise obscure to the readers. The 'midrash' in Ephesians 4 proceeds with a description of the unifying gifts and offices in the church in 4.11–12. The goal of the church's unity is then set out in 4.13, which is itself elaborated in 4.14–16 in such a way as to reinforce the basic exhortation in 4.1.

THE EXHORTATION SET OUT (4.1–6)

The writer 'beseeches', 'exhorts', 'encourages', 'comforts' or 'warns', not simply as the 'prisoner on behalf of Christ', but also 'prisoner of Christ' (4.1). If there is any significance in the change of expression between Ephesians 3.1 and 4.1, more than the purely stylistic, it is that the ambiguity of the genitive – expressing both captivity for the sake of Christ and also captivity to Christ – has become a more consciously 'religious' imprisonment as the text construes not only Paul's understanding of his sufferings (as in Colossians 1.24), but also a developed theology of the vindication of the suffering apostle.

The virtue of 'humility' (4.2) is striking. Josephus (*Jewish War* 4.494) and Epictetus (3.24.56) used the word in the sense of 'meanness of spirit', and it was no virtue at all. However, the word is 'baptized' in Christian writers, so that, according to John Chrysostom, it is that virtue which is displayed 'whenever someone who is great humbles himself' (Migne, PG 62 ad loc.), while for Trench (1860: 179ff.) it is 'esteeming ourselves small, inasmuch as we are so'.

This humility is expressed in 'meekness' (4.2), which is clearly not meekness towards God, for that would be irrelevant to the context, but is rather courtesy, considerateness or meekness towards other people (Arndt and Gingrich 1957: 705). Such behaviour necessarily involves 'longsuffering', as is indicated by the repetition of 'with', by which some parallelism to the preceding clause is indicated. 'Steadfastness' is slowness in avenging wrongs, as in 1 Corinthians 13.4. The obvious significance of these virtues is that they obliterate division and make unity a fact of practical living. By the submission of the church members to each other, unity is maintained.

The phrase 'bearing one another in love' (4.2) is the first of two participial phrases. This phrase is probably to be understood as referring to that 'brotherly' love among believers which bears testimony to the love of Christ himself, to which reference is made in 1.4,6; 2.4; 3.19; 5.2,25; 6.23. The believers are to bear with, in the sense of 'put up with', each other as with those who are not naturally agreeable. This is the disposition which followers of Christ are to adopt towards one another, for in this way 'unity of spirit' is kept within the bond of peace. Thus the significance of 'bearing' is explained by what follows it.

The second participial phrase, 'striving to maintain the unity of the spirit in the bond of peace' (4.3), indicates a sense of difficulty in practising the virtues of love and unity, according to Barth (1974: 428). However, the unity has to be maintained, not attained, for it is something which has already been secured. Whether the reference to 'unity of spirit' is to the Holy Spirit or the human spirit of the community is a matter of some debate; it is probably unwise to separate the two possibilities. The 'bond of peace' is that which holds fast the unity of the church. In 2.14–17 the peace which is established by Christ is specifically the drawing together of both Jew and Gentile in one body, the church, which, in turn, grows into 'a holy temple in the Lord'. The confidence of the writer's exhortation is thus based upon the fact that the community will have little difficulty keeping the unity within that bond, for it would scarcely be conceivable for unity to exist outside the bond of peace which Christ himself has established. Thus it would seem reasonable to suggest that the unity of spirit is the unity of the community's members, but the human spirit and the Spirit of God are in intimate communion (cf. Romans 8.16–17).

According to some commentators, Ephesians 4.4–6 constitutes a quotation from an early Christian hymn or credal confession. However, Houlden rightly notes that 'most of these statements can be paralleled somewhere in Paul's writings, but nowhere are they heaped together' (1977: 309), and we have already observed (see pp. 44–5 above) that the only hymn in the epistle is probably that in 5.14.

The clause 'just as you were called in one hope of your calling' (4.4) reflects the fundamental teleological thrust of the writer's concern. In Paul, this would doubtless have been eschatological, but this writer makes a notable shift in emphasis since his sights are set, not upon a parousia so much as upon knowing the victory of Christ over the powers of evil – within the experience of life in the church. This is the substance of the hope, which is not an attitude of hopefulness, but rather the objective 'thing hoped for', which is to be the subject of realization in the life of the community. This is spelled out later in 4.13.

For the phrase 'one God and Father of all' (4.6), the nearest comparable passage is 1 Corinthians 12.4–11, and the comparison is instructive. There, it is intended to show that diversity in the possession of gifts is not to lead to envy and strife, for all are gifts of one God. Here, no particular trouble is in mind, unless it is a more general failure to preserve unity in the church. There, unity is seen in the Spirit who distributes gifts; here it is to be discerned in every feature of Christian life, where unity pervades the whole structure of faith, and is rooted in the oneness of God himself.

All this unity is necessarily and essentially dependent upon the oneness of God. Houlden (1977: 309) notes that God's Fatherhood here is not only of the faithful; he is the Father of all, and there is a 'rough trinitarian pattern' – one Spirit, one Lord, one God and Father – in this passage. He also notes a Stoic influence in the idea of God pervading all things. The readers of the epistle are to take seriously their vocation, to the extent that they should live a life which mirrors that to which they are called. The emphasis is on a unity which has already been established by God, and consequently upon the kind of behaviour which will enable it to live and grow.

THE BASIS OF THE EXHORTATION (4.7–12)

In this section a quotation from scripture is used to emphasize the point that God, by the Spirit, has given gifts to the church (4.12). In particular, people have been appointed to offices which are intended to lead the church towards maturity and completion as the living body of Christ.

Unity is created and fostered by the gift of grace, not only to the whole church, but also to each member. In the assertion, 'to each is given grace according to the measure of Christ's giving' (4.7), a distinction is drawn between 'each' and 'all', in order to emphasize this particularity. The verb 'is given' in verse 7 anticipates the 'gave' of the quotation from the Psalm 68.18 which is found in Ephesians 4.8:

> When he ascended on high he led captivity captive,
> He gave gifts to men.

In Ephesians, 'grace' is used in a purely general way both in the opening greeting – 'grace to you and peace' – and in the closing farewell – 'grace be with all those who love our Lord Jesus Christ with love undying' (6.24). It also characterizes the appropriate form of speech for believers ('in order that it may give grace to the hearers', 4.29). In a more specific sense, however, this grace is the subject of praise in the opening Benediction (1.6,7); it is the agent of divine salvation (2.5–8); it also characterizes the new order ushered in by God in Christ and proclaimed by Paul (3.2,7,8) (see also the discussion on p. 60 above). Here in Ephesians 4, grace is given to each, and the gift is of grace itself, not of any particular gift.

The text speaks of 'the measure of the gift of Christ' (4.7), indicating that the gift of grace comes not only from God, as is implied in the use of the passive voice, but also from Christ upon his exaltation to the heavens. It also indicates that the measure in which it is given is according to the will of Christ. It is this assertion of Christ, alongside God, as the originator of the gift that requires the Old Testament quotation and midrash.

The fact that the formula 'therefore it says' (4.8) is used to introduce a quotation, here as in 5.14, constitutes another factor which gives the lie to the view that there are quotations from hymns throughout this epistle. Various possibilities suggest themselves for the subject of the verb 'says'. The most likely alternative is to regard it as simply 'it (i.e. scripture) says', with the possible implication at some level, 'it is written'.

The quotation in 4.8 reverses the meaning of the original text in Psalm 68, and it is the misquoted words which make it applicable in the context. Lindars (1961: 51–6) subjects this passage to considerable scrutiny. He notes the departure of the text from that of the Septuagint as follows:

1 'in a man' is changed to 'among men';
2 The verbs are changed from the second to the third person, though this is probably due only to the needs of the context;
3 The text has 'gave' instead of the original 'received'. This was once thought to be due to the influence of the Targum, the Aramaic paraphrase of the Hebrew scriptures, which has: 'Thou ascendedst up to the firmament, O Prophet Moses, thou tookest captives captive, thou didst teach the words of the law, thou gavest them as gifts to the children of men.' But this accounts for the difference in only one word, and the Targum appears to have no other influence on either the form or the interpretation of the text here. Thus it is probably better to suppose that both the Targum and this passage witness to a Hebrew text which had 'gave' for 'received'. This cannot be proved, however, and is probably a case of coincidence rather than actual dependence.

The reason for this change is not difficult to see, according to Lindars: 'thou hast received gifts among men' is 'too compressed to be understood unambiguously' (1961: 53), but it is easy to think of gifts received for men. Thus the receiving is evidently for the purpose of giving. So 'gifts' suggested its own cognate verb, and the idea of receiving dropped out altogether. The idea of giving dominates the whole context in Ephesians 4, implying that the reading in the quotation has an interpretative motive.

For Lindars, Ephesians 4 is a rewriting of 1 Corinthians 12. The more 'fluid' notion of the Spirit there is in the process of giving way to a more concrete idea throughout the pages of the New Testament. The gifts here are from Christ, not from God or the Holy Spirit, and they are functions of their recipients rather than

manifestations of the one Spirit who gives them. There is significance here in the change from 'in a man' to 'to men' in that 'we
are here close to the concrete idea of a gift in the exact sense of
the word', which is reached in the Lucan literature (1961: 57). This
interpretation is broadly in line with that of Schnackenburg (1982:
110–11), who considers that the writer probably found the text in
this form, rather than adapted it for his own purposes.

Some scholars ask the question, Is the passage talking about the
incarnation, or the crucifixion, or something else? Caird (1964)
sees a reference here to the descent of the Spirit at Pentecost; Psalm
68 was, after all, a Pentecost Psalm, as Kirby (1968) points out.
Houlden (1977: 310–11) follows Caird in understanding the descent
as Pentecost, and points out that the ascent 'far above all heavens'
involves a reference to contemporary cosmology, with the realm of
God high beyond all the rest (cf. Hebrews 4.14). The purpose of
the ascent is 'that he might fill all things'. The use of the word 'he'
emphasizes the identity of the descended and ascended one with
the giver of the gifts. The idea is paralleled in the fourth Gospel,
where the Spirit is said by Jesus to be bestowed both by the Father
(John 14.26; 15.26, 'he who comes from the Father') and by himself
(John 14.18; 15.26, 'whom I shall send to you'). Here the gifts are
not faculties given to individuals, but offices within the church, and
the gifts are for all the time of the church's life.

The list of gifts (4.11) refers back to the verb 'he gave' in v. 8.
Houlden compares this list with that in 1 Corinthians 12.4–11,
27–30, and, as we have noted, Lindars is of the opinion that this
passage in Ephesians 4 was written with 1 Corinthians 12 in mind.
The first three titles in 1 Corinthians 12.28 reappear here, 'but this
similarity is overshadowed by important differences in both content
and meaning' according to Houlden (1977: 312). First, the list in
1 Corinthians is longer and more diverse; second, it is a list of
spiritual gifts exercised in the church, whereas Ephesians 4 is a list
of offices. He argues that we may therefore conclude that organ-
ization of the church was simpler and more formal in this community than in the churches of Paul's day. This ties in with what we
know of ministry in the church at a later period from, for example,
the pastoral epistles.

Is this 'anachronism' deliberate? The title of 'apostle' was
associated with authority, and Houlden claims there is a difference
in the use of the term at the beginning of Paul's own letters and
Ephesians 1.1, where this is a claim to authority. However the use

of the title is also a claim to authority in Paul's own letters (von Campenhausen 1969: 33). Ephesians is looking back to a time when apostles (and Paul in particular) were authoritative figures, yet writing for a day in which the authority of these now dead people had to be maintained; hence his insistence upon Paul's authority in Ephesians 3.

'Prophets' are linked with apostles in 2.20 and 3.5 as belonging to the church's earliest days. But there existed also a prophetic ministry within the church at the time of Ignatius (Philadephians 7). The writer probably regarded himself as a prophet – continuing the apostolic tradition, while speaking an authoritative word in interpretation of the gospel for his own day.

'Evangelists' are referred to in the New Testament only here, in Acts 21.8, and in 2 Timothy 4.5 – in other words, only in post-Pauline documents. One wonders how, then, they are to be regarded as 'those who concern themselves with the church's mission to the world' (Mitton 1974: 150). The view that 'an evangelist is presumably one whose task is to spread the gospel' (Houlden 1977: 313) is, of course, widely held. However, the evidence within the pages of the New Testament for the task of evangelists is very scanty, and in view of the later giving of this title to the assumed writers of the Gospels, one wonders whether their name might in fact originate in their telling of stories of Jesus, not necessarily in a context of mission to the world, but rather in that of the church's own liturgical and pedagogical practice.

'Pastor', i.e. 'shepherd', is an image which is applied to Christ in the fourth Gospel. In the Pauline communities it is presumably the same as that of 'overseer' or 'bishop' in Philippians 1.1. 'Teachers', who are mentioned along with them here – (and the implication is, presumably, that they are to be regarded as holding the two offices, or that the one office combines the two functions) – are either instructors of new members, and treated as a single group with pastors, or those who provided general teaching for the community, in such a way that did not differentiate between 'teaching' and 'pastoring'.

The purpose of the giving of the gifts (4.12) is for the equipment of 'the saints' for the fulfilment of two aims: first, for service (cf. the role of Paul as servant of the gospel in 3.7), and second for building up the body of Christ. Thus the whole existence of the church, enabled by God and Christ to serve and to grow into what it is to become, is focused upon its own well-being and unity. To serve is to build up the body, so that it may grow in service.

By calling upon the Jewish scriptures to underline this ethical exhortation, Ephesians is able to point to the existence in the church of those whose task it is specifically to move the church towards the goal of the 'summing up' in Christ. The opening verses of the exhortation referred back to God's act in creating unity. By introducing the subject of office bearers, he is able, obliquely, to recall the readers' minds to the person of the apostle Paul, who was the particular focus of attention in Ephesians 3. His work is carried on by those who are entrusted by God with the care of the community.

THE GOAL OF THE EXHORTATION: THE PERFECT MAN (4.13–16)

The goal of the ethic of Ephesians is the 'summing up' of all things in Christ. The intention of the 'worthy walk' is the bringing to pass in the life of the church of what God intends for Christ and his body, and the words 'until we all attain to unity of faith and of knowledge of the son of God, to a perfect man, to the measure of the stature of the fulness of Christ' (4.13) indicate that a period of development is involved in the church's growth to fulness. The end of the world is less imminent here than it is for Paul.

Barth (1974: 489–96), curiously, translates the verb 'attain' as 'till we meet'. He regards this section as referring to the Pauline understanding of the parousia, when Christians would 'meet the Lord in the air' (1 Thessalonians 4.17). This is very odd, however, and at variance with the thrust of the ethical material as a whole. A developmental understanding of church growth is more likely here.

The occurrence of 'all' in Ephesians 3.9, meaning 'all humanity', suggests that it could mean the same here, or it could equally refer to all Christians. It seems most likely in this context that 'all Christians' are the immediate concern, though it should be borne in mind that the writer is concerned for humanity as a whole, so that the word also carries the connotation of the whole of humanity in principle. That 'unity of faith' is part of the goal of the Christian community would, however, favour the former interpretation.

It is clear, though, from the phrase 'to unity of faith' (4.13), that unity is the central focus of the ethic of this epistle. Everything is geared towards its realization. Unity is, first, of 'faith'. Whether this is 'the faith', or of 'faithfulness', or, perhaps, of something like 'commitment' is not clear, though the first alternative is the most likely, in view of the writer's concern for the primacy of the experience of belief. However, this unity is linked, secondly, to that of 'knowledge of the Son of God' (4.13). Presumably this knowledge is related to what is said about Christ in Ephesians 2, namely, that it is he who is the agent of unity, both between God and humanity, and between Jew and Gentile. Knowledge is that which starts in baptism and which is continued in the experience and behaviour of the believers and the church.

The phrase 'to a perfect man' uses the word which means male, virile and, possibly, fighting. This allusion paves the way for the image of the armour at the conclusion of the letter in 6.10ff. In that passage the ultimate 'summing up' is reached; the military man, integral and complete, and embodying the church, grows into the fulness of the glory of God 'in the heavenlies'.

The 'measure of the stature of the fulness of Christ' (4.13) is either the fulness which comes from Christ to his body, or it is the fulness which Christ has received from the Father (cf. 1.23). In either case believers are to share the stature of this fulness; they are to indwell the great cosmic man, who is Christ. The language has spatial as well as relational overtones. Clearly, the cosmology here is not developed into the kind of 'Gnosticism' such as appears in later Christian history, but this can be seen as a stage along the way to that development.

The way of unity is one of growth to perfection; growth is not elsewhere a New Testament theme, but is peculiar to Ephesians. The reference to 'children' suggests Paul's irritation with the immaturity of the Corinthians in 1 Corinthians 3.1, where children argue among themselves; here in Ephesians 4.14 they are swayed from sound doctrine, and they are being 'carried hither and thither' and 'tossed about like waves'. It is possible that 'false teaching' in some form is beginning to be perceived as a danger here, but it is too early in the church's history for this to be Gnosticism. The reference is more likely to be a rhetorical device which responds to a general fear of wavering; it serves as a warning against the 'unscrupulous' who might want to exploit them by 'trickery, cunning, scheming and error' (Zerwick and Grosvenor 1980).

Ephesians 4.15 has very close parallels with Colossians 2.19. In Colossians, growth comes from God, through Christ, the head, whereas in Ephesians Christ is both the source of growth and its goal. Images of both body and building are combined here, as in Ephesians 4.12, with the latter predominant. The phrase 'in love' occurs twice in the two verses, to emphasize the concern for unity, and it echoes the similar use of the expression in Ephesians 1.4 (see p. 47 above).

The exhortation included in the participle 'truthing it' is not simply 'speaking the truth', but 'being utterly genuine, sincere and honest'. Abbott (1897: 123) suggests 'cherishing the truth in love'; this includes 'doing the truth' (John 3.21). The 'truth' is that of the gospel outlined in this epistle, and love is its inevitable corollary. 'The truth as it is in Jesus' is to be understood as baptismal instruction, which is related to teaching, which comes from Jesus and which acknowledges the primacy of his baptism.

The notion of growth (4.16) is not, as we have just noted, a particularly Pauline term, nor is it to be found in the Gospels. This is hardly a matter of surprise, in view of the expectation of the imminent end, but it is a particular feature of Ephesians. However, this growth is not a question of 'looking unto Jesus', as in Hebrews 12.2, as Mitton suggests (1976: 157), since here the emphasis is on some kind of incorporation into him. Growth is to take place into that which is the source of the believers' life and which they already indwell – the cosmic body of Christ.

In Ephesians 4.16 the emphasis on the totality of the church is restated. It is perceived as a unity comprising several joints and limbs, after concentration on the diverse gifts and offices. There follows an extended description of the way in which those joints and limbs which make up the body are fitted and joined together by what is supplied to each part, so that the body may grow in love. Again, the 'head' is the 'beginning' or 'source' of the body. Believers 'grow up into him' as the archetypal image of the second Adam is realized in them. This growth is something to which the community contributes by 'cherishing truth (that is, the truth of Paul's gospel as presented in Ephesians 2) in love'.

The 'worthy walk' (4.1) is to be taken up because it leads to the fulfilment of God's plan for humankind's perfection. It is facilitated by the Spirit's gifts to the church in baptism (and the initiative of God in this is attested by scripture). These 'gifts' (4.11) are the members themselves with their different functions and offices, under the leadership of those whose function it is to care for the church's growth. The members combine to produce an organic body which cultivates love (4.15–16), the very medium in which the church lives and grows, and to which it owes its origin. The first 'walk' section thus demonstrates the writer's concern that the promised 'summing up' should be enacted in the life of the community – by a walk which is worthy of the believers' calling, and which fosters unity.

Chapter 6

Walk differently, in love and in light

As we have suggested, the ethical section of Ephesians (4.1–6.9) develops by the use five times of the verb 'walk'. This 'ethic' constitutes the human response to the 'grace' of God as it has been expounded in this letter. The present chapter of this book examines three further exhortations based upon this verb, in 4.17–5.14. The believers are urged to walk: first, 'no longer . . . like the Gentiles'; second, 'in love'; and finally, 'as children of light'. This whole section of the epistle develops in such a way that there is a constant dynamic throughout the individual exhortations, so that each one leads into the next. A particular feature of this ethical material is the lists of vices and virtues. We shall discuss these after an examination of the text.

WALK DIFFERENTLY

The exhortation to walk 'no longer as the Gentiles' extends from 4.17 to 5.1. In this section the text expounds in negative terms the style of life according to which 'the Gentiles' walk, and contrasts this with the 'worthy walk' of those who are called to faith in Christ. As in the exhortation in Ephesians 4.1–16, the underlying call is to unity, and the assumption is that the Gentiles do not walk this way, but that their lifestyle is its very antithesis. 'Darkness of mind' and 'alienation from God' (4.18) do not make for unity, so those who are held, as it were, in thrall to these vices are consequently antagonistic, along with the forces of darkness and alienation, to God's purpose in the 'summing up' of all things in Christ.

The exhortation to walk differently is introduced as Paul's 'testimony', or 'witness' (literally, 'This therefore I say and testify in the Lord', 4.17). This 'testimony' places a moral obligation upon those who hear it, and becomes an 'exhortation upon the basis of testimony'. The expression 'in the Lord' recalls the readers' minds to the apostle's imprisonment for the Lord's sake (3.1; 4.1); this exhortation is to be regarded as 'in the Lord', just as Paul's imprisonment was. The expression 'the Gentiles' (4.17) signified simply 'the nations' in the Septuagint, but came later to indicate 'the nations' as distinct from the nation of Israel. The word is used in Ephesians 2.11 and 3.1 of Gentiles as distinct from Jews. As Schnackenburg points out, however, it is used here in a most derogatory sense, for it signifies the radical contrast between an understanding of life based upon God, and a completely rootless existence (1982: 129).

The act of clothing

The 'difference' in lifestyle to be expected in the readers is expressed in the image of the act of changing clothes. The metaphor of clothing is used in 4.22–4 to distinguish 'the old man' from 'the new man', and the style of life recommended corresponds with the action of 'putting off' (4.22, repeated in 4.25) the old and 'putting on' (4.24) the new. 'The old' therefore belongs to the Gentiles' former existence, when they were aliens from Israel and strangers to God (2.11–22); this 'old' manner of life is in the process of decay, which echoes the language of death in 2.1–10. The 'new man' is 'being created according to God in righteousness, holiness and truth'. Such a transformation is brought about by renewal in the 'spirit of the mind'. Hence the writer's instruction, 'be renewed by the spirit of your mind'.

The use of the verbs 'take off' and 'put on' suggests a number of possible backgrounds: apocalyptic literature, mystery religions and the Jewish scriptures, both Hebrew and Greek – imagery which was popular in later, Gnostic, texts. Two other Pauline passages, Romans 13.12–14 and Galatians 3.27, make use of such imagery, as do Hebrews 12.1 and 1 Peter 2.1. A whole range of possible backgrounds lies behind clothing metaphors in the religious parlance of the day. In view of the language concerning 'learning Christ' and 'the truth as it is in Jesus' (which are discussed later), it would appear likely that the moment of baptism is in mind. Thus what is significant is that, whatever its ritual background, the writer uses clothing imagery here to refer to a style of living and behaviour which reflects the moral change brought about by faith in Christ, which is expressed in baptism. The clothing which the readers are to 'put off' is said in Ephesians 4.22 to be the 'old man', in order that they may be able to 'put on' the 'new man' of 4.24. It is this contrast that characterizes the distinction the writer wishes to draw between the 'walk', or manner of life, of the Gentiles, and that which is to be pursued by the believers. The writer is concerned to place some emphasis on change and newness.

The state of the 'old man'

The 'old man' is to be regarded as synonymous with 'Gentile' conduct. The Gentiles are regarded as living in 'vanity of mind' – or 'spirit' – (4.17), and this was a general view of paganism among the Jews (cf., for example, Isaiah 44.12–20). It covers not only the transitory, contingent nature of life, but also the emptiness of human striving apart from God (Abbott 1897: 129). The word is used in Psalm 94.11, 'The Lord knows the thoughts of men, that they are vain', which Paul quotes in 1 Corinthians 3.20. In fact, Paul makes much use of this concept in Romans 1.19–21, which has close affinities to this passage. Schnackenburg sums this up by saying, 'Vanity of mind' is more than intellectual ignorance: it is a mentally "locked up" existence' (1982: 200).

This passage in Ephesians quite deliberately brings the whole mental consciousness of 'the Gentiles' under consideration; their darkened understanding fails to comprehend the truth, and their state of alienation from 'the life of God' (4.18) is evidenced in their behaviour. Bengel notes, *vita spiritualis accenditur in credentibus ex ipsa Dei vita* ('the spiritual life of believers is warmed from the true life of God', quoted in Abbott 1897: 129–30).

Paul in Romans 1.24,26,28 regards the Gentiles as having been 'given up' by God to even grosser moral excesses. In this passage in Ephesians, because of their 'lack of feeling', or 'hardness of heart', they wilfully and blindly devote themselves to 'licentiousness, greedy to practise every kind of uncleanness'. As the element of Gentile wilfulness is emphasized, the note of God's judgment is weakened. What has happened to the Gentiles has been the result of their own blind choice. The view expressed here is not so much one of condemnation – though that idea is not entirely absent – as one of a pity which issues in compassion. It remains clear, however, that the Gentiles' way of life is quite out of keeping with the life of faith in Christ.

Moreover, because of their hardness of heart, the Gentiles are beyond feeling, and they willingly devote themselves to 'debauchery', which the writer further characterizes with the words 'greedy to practise every kind of uncleanness'. The expression *en pleonexia* probably means here simply that they carry out these practices 'to excess' (Zerwick and Grosvenor 1980: 586).

After listing these Gentile vices, the writer uses one of his most striking phrases in his reminder to the readers of their initiation and life in the church: 'But you did not so learn Christ' (4.20). This significant phrase has inevitably given rise to some degree of comment on the part of scholars. Either the learning took place when the gospel was first preached, or this is a reference to the moral demand implicit in such preaching. 'Hearing' and 'being taught' (4.21) are obviously important. Clearly, 'learning Christ' is something that has taken place in the past, and is common to all of the readers. In the light of what follows, and the appeal which the writer makes to the readers' experience, there must presumably be some reference to an experience of Christ which is common to the readers of the letter – and this can hardly be anything other than the experience of Christ by the Spirit in the rite of baptism (Conzelmann 1962: 80; Abbott 1897: 131).

This view is supported by a consideration of the equally striking statement which follows: 'as the truth is in Jesus' (4.21). In what sense is 'the truth' to be found 'in' Jesus? Some scholars are of the opinion that what is meant here is something akin to an understanding of truth which is 'done', as in John 3.21, and is thus closely related to holiness. Abbott regards it as obedience to the practical teaching of Jesus (1897: 135). It seems unlikely, however, that this could be a reference to a tradition of teaching going back to Jesus himself; it is most probably a reference to baptism in the name of Jesus. This is borne out by the content of what is 'put on' in the verses which follow (4.22–4). From a focus upon the negative picture of the 'old man' which is to be discarded, the writer turns to the image of the 'new man', which the believers have 'put on' in baptism, and to which they are to give constant expression in the way they live their lives. Such a lifestyle is the practical expression of the 'Pauline' gospel of the 'summing up' of all things which was expounded in the first part of the epistle.

The nature of the 'new man'

The 'new man' is what the believers are to 'put on', and this new man contrasts with the old, whose character has been portrayed in the foregoing verses. The participle 'putting off' in 4.25 takes up the use of the same verb in 4.22. The first vice to be 'put away' is 'falsehood', and this is elaborated with a reference to Zechariah 8.16, 'This is what you must do: speak the truth to each other, administer true and sound justice in your courts.'

The 'new man' is one who has put away 'falsehood'. But why should the first exhortation be to avoid falsehood, and why should this text be chosen in order to underline it? The first question is answered by the observation that the writer is concerned that falsehood destroys unity; 'for we are members of one another' is the explanation given. This mutuality of membership is to be rooted in an understanding of membership of Christ's body. This was an ethical matter for Paul (cf. Robinson 1952), and is no less so for the writer of Ephesians, whose understanding of unity is derived from the conviction that it is the will of God to unite, renew and bring all things together in Christ. The answer to the second question is found in the Zechariah text's suitability here. The verse in Zechariah occurs within the context of a passage which is concerned about the rebuilding of the Temple – this accords well with the Temple imagery earlier in the epistle – which also was an image of organic unity and growth.

The quotation in Ephesians 4.26 from Psalm 4.4 ('Be angry and do not sin') seems to fit uneasily into the context. There are those who say that the verb should be translated as in the Authorized Version and Revised Version, 'stand in awe'; this translation is improbable, however, in view of the fact that there is no succeeding 'before me', or some such phrase. The meaning of the verb is, more naturally, 'be angry', as in the Revised Version margin and the Revised Standard Version, and the imperative is to be taken as permissive rather than as a command. The Gospels have references to Jesus's being angry; anger is only sinful if it gets out of proportion. The commands, 'Do not let the sun go down on your wrath' and 'do not give place to the devil', suggest that angry feelings should not be so indulged that they lead to malice. The command that the thief is to 'steal no more' (4.28) does not necessarily suggest the presence of theft among the community; this is a rhetorical expression to encourage hard work for the sake of the possibility of giving to others.

Moving on from falsehood and theft, the text addresses the way in which the 'new man' should speak. Conversation should not be *sapros*, meaning 'rotten' or 'diseased' (4.29), but 'edifying . . . that it may impart grace'. The most likely meaning of 'grace' here is 'benefit', and there are parallels for this elsewhere in the New Testament, for example 2 Corinthians 1.15 and 8.6. The readers are to beware of 'grieving the Holy Spirit of God', in whom the believers were 'sealed' (4.30) at baptism. There is perhaps an eschatological reference here, in that 'sealing' points on to the coming of the Lord (Lampe 1967: 3–7).

There follows (in 4.31) a further list of vices which are to be avoided, all of which would gnaw at the vitals of a community's life: 'bitterness' is the refusal to be reconciled; 'wrath' is the temporary excitement of passion, to be contrasted with 'anger' which is more settled; 'clamour' and 'slander' (not 'blasphemy') generate ill-will (cf. Colossians 3.8); 'malice' is evil intention. All of these vices clearly make for discord among the members of the community and are therefore to be avoided. The believers are exhorted to kindness, tenderness and forgiveness – because God in Christ has forgiven them.

In 5.1 the exhortation reaches the point at which the 'new man' is acknowledged as Christ. On this basis the believers are to behave towards one another in the same way as God, in Christ, has treated them; they are to become 'imitators of God'. The theme of 'imitation' occurs frequently in antiquity, in philosophy, in poetry and in art, and was celebrated by Auerbach (1968). The closest the Bible comes to the idea of 'imitating God' is with the command to imitate God's holiness in Leviticus 11.44, which is quoted by Paul in Romans 1.7 (cf. Barth 1974: 555); the idea appears only here in the New Testament. The meaning of the command here is clear from the preceding exhortation to mercy, forgiveness and love – that this is the way to unity and peace. The command to be 'kind, tenderhearted and forgiving' – just as God in Christ has forgiven – leads on naturally to the appeal to become 'imitators of God'. Thus all these instructions lead up to the beginning of the next section, with the command to 'walk in love' of Ephesians 5.2; the mention of God's forgiveness leads to the command to imitate God, and 'walk in love'.

The text therefore sets out specific virtues in order to promote a very practical unity within the life of the Christian community. The 'summing up' of all things is brought to effect in the simple

and loving way that human beings treat each other within the
community of those who know themselves to be the objects of the
prior reconciliation of humanity with God. Read historically, the
text suggests that the community was in danger, either of lapsing
from its faith, or of losing heart. An alternative reading would
suggest that the prohibitions stand on purely literary grounds. The
text expands Colossians 3.5ff. for the sake of the literary effect, so
the emphasis is not so much on the immoral deeds of unsaved
Gentiles, but on the virtues which are to be expected in the lives of
all who walk the way of Christ.

WALK IN LOVE

The command, 'Therefore become imitators of God' (5.1) sums
up the previous passage and makes possible the transition to the
command 'walk in love' (5.2). The statement may be paralleled in
1 Corinthians 11.1 and 4.16. To imitate God 'as beloved children'
is clearly to fulfil the exhortation set out in that earlier passage by
a life of goodness, mercy and mutual love. This love is itself
foreshadowed in the adjective applied to the readers, 'beloved'.
Christ's death is here regarded as some kind of offering, or
sacrifice. Sacrificial terminology lies in the Hebraism underlying
'for an aroma of fragrance' (cf. Exodus 29.18, Leviticus 2.9), and
the way Christ is said to have 'given himself for us' as an act of love.

The parallel passage in Colossians occurs in the context of the
exhortation 'seek the things which are above' (Colossians 3.1).
Ephesians elaborates the exhortation in Colossians. The 'putting
on' and 'putting off' imagery remains, but the virtues in Colossians
are simply listed as those of tolerance, forgiveness, love and peace;
there follow some instructions about the community's worship, and
then the household code (see chapter 7 below), before the final
exhortation to prayer and the closing greetings. Ephesians creates
a piece of ethical exhortation of greater range and significance; it
is a conscious, stylized piece of writing, in keeping with both the
liturgical setting of the epistle, and its intention to produce a
memorial to a beloved apostle.

The ending of this passage emphasizes the movement on the
next level of exhortation – 'be kind to one another, tender-hearted
and forgiving one another, even as God in Christ has forgiven you.
Become therefore imitators of God, like beloved children, and walk
in love' (4.31–5.2). In this way, as has been said, Ephesians 5.1

functions as a bridge between this exhortation and what follows. The text now urges its readers quite specifically to walk in love, and perhaps it is not surprising that 'fornication' (5.3), along with its attendant vices of 'impurity' and 'covetousness' (this last now to be taken in its substantive sense, unlike its occurrence in the phrase in 4.19), should be the first vice to be avoided here, because sexual misbehaviour, though linked to loving, is the obvious antithesis to the love which the readers are to practise. Impurity and covetousness both involve inordinate desire (Houlden 1977: 324), but there may also be a link here with the ten commandments, and the passage is very close at this point to Colossians 3.5, 'put to death, therefore, those parts of you which are earthly, fornication, impurity, passion, evil desire and covetousness, which is idolatry'. There are ritual associations to impurity; and riches, fornication and profanation of the Temple are held together in the Damascus Document at Qumran (Vermes 1962: 101). In saying that such vices are not so much as to be named among them, Ephesians sets out an absolute command that their behaviour should be such that the very idea of such vices should not enter people's minds when they reflect upon the life of the community of the saints.

The further list of vices is designed to heighten the writer's instruction that the readers should spend their time 'giving thanks' (5.4), for this will keep their attention from wandering from the goal to which they have been set. 'Filthiness', 'silly talk' and 'levity' are 'not fitting' for saints. The concept of what is 'fitting' clearly has Stoic undertones, but its emphasis here, of course, is upon what is fitting for those who believe in Christ; the appropriate lifestyle is one of thanksgiving. Perhaps there is a distant reference to the church's worship in the Eucharist here, given the sacrificial nature of the language in 5.2, and the reference to worship a few verses later.

The sharp admonition in 5.5, 'For know this, that no fornicator, or impure person, or one who is covetous, that is an idolater, has any inheritance in the kingdom of Christ and of God', serves to indicate the strictest separation between the 'saints' and the Gentile world which they have now left. All the types of evil person listed have already had their particular vice attacked in the previous section. Ephesians 5.6–7 urges the readers to have nothing to do with such evil, and expresses here the statement which comes closest to an eschatology, 'for it is because of these things that the wrath of God comes upon the children of disobedience' (5.6). This statement is in the present tense, and raises the question, when does this act of judgment take place? In the present, or in the future? According to Paul, the wrath of God has already been revealed – in the gospel as it is preached (Romans 1.18, cf. Colossians 3.6). It could be that the wrath of God is regarded here in Ephesians as yet to be revealed, or, more probably, this is an imprecise statement of what is, by the time of this epistle, conventional teaching on the issue.

The radical nature of the divide between the readers and their former existence is underlined by the following reference to the contrast between light and darkness. It is possible that some form of Greek dualism is to be seen here, but in fact it is more likely to be of Jewish origin, with links at Qumran. The readers are to behave in accordance with what they are, and walk as children of light; this represents a moral, rather than a metaphysical, dualism.

WALK IN LIGHT

The fourth instance of the verb 'walk' (Ephesians 5.8) is introduced by an expansion of the moral dualism of the preceding section. The readers are reminded of their previous nature as 'darkness', and on this basis are urged, since they are now 'light', to walk as children of the light and to bring forth its fruit.

The virtues that are to be expected of those who walk as the 'children of light' are 'goodness, righteousness and truth' (5.9). That 'light' should bear 'fruit' is a striking image. Since the kind of dualism present here is clearly not of a metaphysical variety, but presents rather two ways of living, it is clearly appropriate as a way of referring to the kind of life which will manifest itself in moral goodness, and is reminiscent of the kind of language that Paul uses concerning the result of the Spirit's indwelling in Galatians 5.22.

The children of light are those who understand – or 'work out', or 'estimate' – what is 'pleasing to the Lord' (5.10). The word 'pleasing' is used in Stoic literature, but here in Ephesians the emphasis broadens out from 'what is fitting' to what is pleasing to God. At all events, there is an element of care to be taken in the working out of an appropriate way of life. The participle used for 'work out' or 'estimate' here is difficult to translate: the Revised Standard Version has 'trying to learn', and Abbott (1897: 153) has 'putting to the proof, partly by thought and partly by experience'. In Romans 12.2 Paul urges the Romans to 'test', or 'discover by putting to the test', what is the will of God. This 'testing' involves the avoidance of the works of those who are still in darkness, which are themselves regarded as belonging to the darkness.

The exhortation in 5.11, 'but instead, expose, or reprove, them' is also a difficult phrase. It seems to provide evidence of links with the behaviour of the Essene community at Qumran, where faults on the part of members of the community were 'reproved' by the whole community – though here it is the deeds, not the person, who are the object of reproof. The verb is very wide in meaning, and may mean 'convict', 'expose' or 'bring to light'. Here, the works of darkness are exposed, and therefore condemned, by being contrasted with the good works of the believers.

The statement 'for it is a shame even to speak of the things that they do in secret' (5.12) highlights the sense of shame to be encouraged in the readers at the sinfulness of the world from which believers are to turn away. The following verse gives the reason for this; the evil deeds of the Gentiles will be brought to light and 'reproved' by the light. Consequently, believers are to be seen to have no part in that which the light of God will ultimately reveal to be totally alien to them and to himself. To say 'for anything that becomes visible is light' (5.14) appears a little curious, and it is probably to be taken simply as an observation that whatever is visible is so because light shines upon it. There is a sense in which the light which the believers enjoy, which comes from God, will inevitably also bring to light the deeds of those who walk in darkness – this is thus a restatement of the exhortation in Ephesians 5.11, 'but rather reprove them'.

This exhortation in Ephesians 5.11–13 thus sums up the preceding verses, and it is expanded so that it paves the way for the quotation from the hymn in 5.14:

'Awake, O sleeper,
and arise from the dead,
and Christ shall give you light.'

That this is a hymn is clear from the way it is introduced. The origin of the quotation may be found in Isaiah 61.1. Deuteronomy 33.2, at the beginning of the Song of Moses, speaks of the Lord coming from Sinai; Psalm 50.2 speaks of God 'shining out from Sion'; and Colossians 3.4 contains the promise 'when Christ, who is our life, shall appear, then shall we also appear with him in glory'. These all seem tenuous as possible sources for this hymnic saying, but they do indicate a similar line of thought. The hymn presumably derives from the worship of the community, and is used in this context, not only to highlight the call to a way of life which will not earn the rebuke of the believing community, but also to point forward to the promise of light which has yet to dawn in the person of Christ.

The way of life – or 'worthy walk' – urged by the writer is thus distinguished from that of the Gentiles. It involves the removal of the old and the donning of the new; believers are called to a renewed existence in the light of the resurrection of Christ. This life is naturally to be regarded as characterized by love, and as a demonstration of the light of Christ's glory, which is revealed supremely in the 'summing up' of all things.

WALKING

The exhortations based on 'walk' become shorter after the first two. They take up the material in Colossians, adapting it for a particular theological purpose. However, the material is here largely for the sake of its form, and this form becomes a little unwieldy; it is difficult to retain the fine sense of the epistle's structure in these sections. It is significant to note how all of this paraenesis promotes an ethic of unity. This is a point of major significance for Ephesians, since this is clearly one of the prime concerns of the writer of the epistle. The essential unity of the church, which is part of God's ultimate plan, is to be reflected in the practical unity of those who believe. The ethic set out here is one of unity, and it gives expression to the 'summing up' of all things in Christ, since bringing together in unity is one of the possible ranges of meaning for the verb 'to sum up' which was established earlier.

The structure of this whole passage is based upon the call to the 'worthy walk' urged in Ephesians 4.1. Some progress of thought may be noted here. First, there is an obvious emphasis on unity, and the behaviour of the community is to reflect a consciousness of the 'summing up' which God both has achieved, and is in the process of achieving, through Christ. Second, there is a progression of imagery through the 'walk' sections, beginning with 'worthiness', which is to be contrasted with the lifestyle of the Gentiles, and reflecting both the love and the light of God in Christ. This represents an original application of the text of Colossians. Ephesians sets out a theological and ethical position and, in the 'household code', covers the whole spectrum of social relationships as they would be understood in its day.

NOTE ON 'VICES AND VIRTUES'

As we noted above, the use of lists of vices and virtues is characteristic of much of the material discussed in this chapter. They
serve to highlight the contrast between 'Gentile' life and the life
of love and light which the readers are urged to lead. Such lists are
a prominent feature of New Testament ethical instruction, and
may be found also in other passages: Matthew 5.3–12; Romans
1.19–32, 13.12–14; 1 Corinthians 5.9–11, 6.9–10; 2 Corinthians
6.14–7.1; Galatians 5.19–23; Colossians 3.5–17; 1 Timothy 1.9–10,
3.2–12; 2 Timothy 3.2–5, 16–17; Revelation 21.7–8, 22.14–15; as
well as in 1 Clement 62.2. Barth (1974: 551) gives expression to the
widely held view that they are designed primarily for the instruction of the newly converted, although he thinks that 'virtue' is not
an appropriate word for them, since it is a philosophical term
which is not sufficiently theological; he would rather use the
expression 'good works'.

Many scholars have explored the possible origin of these catalogues of vices and virtues. Preisker (1949) compared the catalogues
with Jewish and Stoic parallels and saw 'love' as the root principle
in the New Testament lists, though he left unanswered the question
as to what 'virtue' or 'vice' might mean when applied to the
behaviour of a Christian. Vögtle (1936: 232–3) examined the virtue
and vice lists in the New Testament, with particular reference to
the church's mission, and compared them with ethical catalogues
in hellenistic, Old Testament and contemporary Jewish literature.
Selwyn (1947: 459ff.) saw two traditions: a 'Christian Holiness
Code' and the baptismal catechism of the early church. He noted
the connection between this Code and the Apostolic Decree of Acts
15, but considered that baptismal catechism was related to a later
stage, when relations between Jewish and Gentile Christians were
not so pressing, and other problems presented themselves. Dinkler
(1952) drew attention to the writings of Stoics and contemporary
Judaism, and emphasized that, for Paul, christology and eschatology
implied ethics. Wibbing (1959) made a major study of the ethical
lists and traced their origin from both secular and religious sources.
He was of the opinion that, in view of the difficulty in proving Jewish
antecedents, Greek literature was all the more to be examined. He
noted that both Bultmann (1910) and Bonhöffer (1911) point to
Stoic influences. Lietzmann (1933) saw parallels in the Stoics and
in Philo, and Dibelius and Greeven (1953) saw a link with the

doctrine of the 'Two Ways'. He noted the absence from the catalogues of any theological emphasis, and observed that, for Judaism and in New Testament writers, duties are not derived from man, but from God and his Law. Easton (1932) attempted to establish the independence of New Testament lists of virtues and vices from Greek or Jewish examples according to whether sins are of 'act' or of 'disposition'.

The most recent major study on this subject is that of Kamlah (1964). He lists two types of catalogue: one which registers good and evil deeds, with a promise of blessing or the threat of destruction; and another which lists the vices and virtues, but then supplements them with exhortations to 'strip off' and 'put on' evil and good respectively. The origin of these is to be found in Iranian sources, he says, and also in Plato, Aristotle, Stoicism, Wisdom literature, the Qumran community, Philo, Jewish apocryphal writings and the Jewish and Christian doctrine of the Two Ways. He argues that Judaism became for early Christianity the mediator of the Iranian doctrine of two opposite spirits vying for the control of man. Jewish thought changed these two spirits into 'angels' or 'ways', in order to avoid a threat to monotheism.

According to Kamlah, Paul 'demythologized' this system further – especially, for example, in Galatians 5.17 – into two subsequent aeons, setting out two correlative modes of being. Baptism was thus the occasion for the admonition and this explains the imagery of putting off and putting on. What is important is the holiness of the congregation, rather than the virtue of the individual, as with the Stoics, for holiness is the essence of the 'new man', the true Adam, the body of Christ. The use of catalogues is thus consonant with the eschatological character of the early Christian proclamation.

Fischer (1973: 147ff.) sees the origin of catalogues of vices and virtues in Jewish missionary propaganda, and draws attention to Wisdom of Solomon 14.22–7, Philo and Aristeas. For him, their basic structure is dualistic, and he thinks it possible that the primitive Christian mission gave it its particular form. Renunciation of the past took place primarily in baptism. He rightly notes that the dualism is not only ethnic – between the baptized and the Gentiles – but also temporal, as is evidenced in Ephesians 2.1–3, and he says that it is impossible to draw concrete conclusions about the actual life of the Gentile Christians addressed.

The parallels indicated in the Jewish scriptures, in Greek philosophy, in Persian religion, in Stoic teaching, in the popular orators, in Philo, at Qumran, in Rabbinic *halakoth*, in Jewish liturgies and in Christian catechetics all indicate, then, that there is a whole range of sources which come together in the New Testament ethical lists. The significance of these lists in Ephesians is not so much their origin as the use to which they are put. Ephesians is clearly heir to all of them, especially the Pauline examples, which bear a highly christological emphasis. The closest source, however, for the writer of Ephesians is clearly the Epistle to the Colossians, which the writer is using as his base.

Why, then, are these lists used? It is clear that the early Christian ethic was christological. Paul's most consistent formula for moral admonition was his phrase 'in Christ', and this was to be understood in an eschatological sense, which in practice meant dependence upon the Spirit of the risen Christ. However, after Paul, as the need grew for the community to continue to live in society and to take it seriously, the early Christians were searching for a form in which to couch their distinctive and developing morality. This would be especially the case at the reflective rather than the casuistic level. Obviously there is danger in over-dramatizing the alleged effect of the delay of the parousia upon the early church, but a sense of the need to go on living in society may be observed also in the 'household codes'.

Chapter 7

Walk wisely

In this chapter we come to a consideration of the fifth and last of these exhortations which are based upon the verb 'walk'. Ephesians has set out an understanding of Paul's gospel in terms appropriate for a later period, and the second half of the epistle lays down the kind of lifestyle which is a suitable response to God's grace in 'summing up' all things in Christ. The readers are urged, 'See therefore how wisely (or, carefully) you walk' (5.15). As with the previous exhortations, they are to conduct their lives in a manner worthy of their calling to reconciliation with God and to unity between Israel and the Gentiles. This fifth exhortation soon develops into a 'household code', which was an established structure in ancient ethical literature. For Ephesians, to walk wisely is to 'be filled with the Spirit'. This exhortation is developed by means of participles into two further commands: to give thanks and to submit to one another.

The exhortation follows the quotation of the hymn (5.14):

'Awake, O sleeper,
And arise from the dead,
And Christ shall give you light.'

The term 'wisely' or 'carefully' (5.15) consequently conjures up the image of a walk appropriate for those who have just been aroused from slumber by the light of a bright morning, for the word translated 'wisely' in most modern English versions, or (perhaps better) by 'circumspectly' in the Authorized Version, may also mean 'precisely' or 'exactly'. This gives the impression of a careful step (perhaps with bleary eyes!) in the face of the light of day. More particularly, the expression contrasts drunkenness, which is a state associated with the night, with a sobriety in life and worship which is more fitting for those who have been awakened to daylight by the risen Christ from the sleep of death.

This is the final occasion on which the verb 'walk' is used in the letter. So the progression in the ethical material indicates that 'walking wisely' is the final emphasis that the text wishes to convey. Wisdom is to be found in the mutual submission which is urged here, and the phrase 'not as foolish, but as wise' (5.15) serves to underline the importance of this. Care is necessary in the way the believers 'walk', because the moment has to be 'redeemed' (5.16); the Revised Version speaks of 'buying up the opportunity'. The emphasis is on the importance of each present moment; 'redeeming the time' is a participial phrase which implies the imperative. 'The days are evil' (5.16), so this is no time for drunkenness. On the contrary, now is the time for the Spirit's fulness in the life of the community, and this is to be evidenced both in its worship, and in the way its members conduct themselves with one another.

The expression 'redeeming the time' (5.16) is used in Colossians 4.5 in the context of the believers' conduct towards those outside the church: 'walk in wisdom to those outside, redeeming the time'. Here in Ephesians, however, the readers are urged to see that the present opportunity – the new day that has dawned with the resurrection – be exploited for demonstrating among themselves all the virtues just outlined. The exhortation, 'therefore do not be unwise, but understand what the will of the Lord is' (5.17), seems repetitive, in view of what has already been said in 5.15, but it serves again to emphasize the wisdom which the 'worthy walk' demands.

With the specific injunction 'do not be drunk with wine, in which is excess, but be filled with the spirit' (5.18), carousing is contrasted with Christian worship. Alcohol was used to induce ecstatic behaviour in religions of the time, and there may be some distant allusion to the Eucharist here. It is also possible that this is a jibe at the excesses of some Christian communities. However, what is most likely, again, is that this is a rhetorical antithesis for the sake of emphasis (cf. Romans 13.13, 1 Thessalonians 5.7; also Proverbs 23.31). There is to be no 'excess' (5.13), but only the sobriety of Spirit-led living.

The expression 'speaking to each other in psalms and hymns and spiritual songs, singing and making melody in your hearts to the Lord' (5.19), is a clear expansion of Colossians 3.16, which has the rather shorter 'with psalms, hymns and spiritual songs singing with love in your hearts to the Lord'. Fulness of the Spirit issues in hymnody and praise to God, whereas excess of wine would result only in drunken carousing. In contrast with Colossians, Ephesians makes a specific point about thanksgiving in worship. It is possible that some eucharistic reference could be present here, even in so early a text, though there is little evidence to suggest that 'giving thanks' had this meaning so early. The verb is used of the Eucharist in *Didache* 9.1–3, Justin, *Apology* I.65.5 and Clement of Alexandria, *Stromateis* 1.19. Nevertheless, it is in the context of the submission of the community to God in worship that the writer is led on to the 'household code', with its particular and distinctive emphasis on the virtue of mutual submission, introduced by the participle 'submitting'.

'Household codes' came to be a widespread convention in ethical writing of the first century, not only among Christian communities, but in Judaism and other contexts in the hellenistic world (Carrington 1940; Hunter 1961). They contain basic moral instruction for the members of the household at their various social levels. There are others elsewhere in the New Testament; this 'household code' in Ephesians is based on that in the Epistle to the Colossians; others are to be found in the letters to Timothy and Titus and in 1 Peter.

The exhortation is introduced in Ephesians 5.21 by the participle 'submitting', which depends, grammatically, on the finite verb 'be filled' in 5.18. As is the case consistently throughout the ethical section of Ephesians, one exhortation gives rise to the next. The participle 'submitting' in 5.21 is thus parallel with the other two participles, 'speaking' in 5.19 and 'giving thanks' in 5.20. Some kind of progression may thus be traced, from the purely liturgical in 'speaking', through that which embraces both liturgical and practical in 'giving thanks', to the purely ethical in 'submitting'.

Submission, then, is the key, and this applies to all the members of the community, which is addressed here in its constituent households; the exhortations are to marriage partners, to children and fathers, and to slaves and masters. What is important, however, is that something different is being said here about all these relationships – especially that of marriage, since that is elaborated in more detail. This should not be pressed too strongly, but the difference consists in the mutuality of the submission urged by the writer of Ephesians, which contrasts with the more 'authoritarian' teaching of the 'household code' in Colossians.

MARRIAGE IN EPHESIANS

Ephesians not only develops further the teaching on the marriage relationship which is to be found in the Epistle to the Colossians, but also sets out thereby an understanding of marriage which is unique in the pages of the New Testament. A number of reasons may adduced to demonstrate this.

The first is that the verb is changed from its finite form in Colossians to a participle – 'submitting'. More especially, its function is altered from an exhortation exclusively to wives in Colossians to an overriding principle of mutual submission governing the whole 'household code' in Ephesians 5.21. Colossians 3.18 has 'Wives, be subject to (submit to) your husbands, as is fitting in the Lord'; and the husbands are exhorted to love their wives, and not be harsh with them. The writer of Ephesians has removed the verb 'submit' from that position and has placed it at the head of the household code, thus altering the significance of relationships within the household in the community he addresses. Thus the Ephesian code elaborates the command expressed in the participle 'submitting' at the head of the section. An examination of the other exhortations also suggests that the exhortation to submission is not restricted to the relationship between husband and wife.

This brings into the discussion again the whole question of the meaning of 'head' and its cognates in the New Testament epistles, which was discussed in the word study in chapter 3 above. Reference was made there to the work of Bedale (1954) in drawing attention to the fact that, in normal usage, the Greek word *kephalê* did not mean 'head' in the sense of 'ruler' or 'chief' of a community. If it has this sense in Paul and other New Testament writers, that is the result of the Septuagint's use of the term to translate the Hebrew *rosh*.

Bedale's article leads to the conclusion that 'head' and 'beginning' became virtually interchangeable, through their association with the Hebrew word *rosh*, even though they have nothing in common in classical Greek. He showed that Paul, in using *kephalê*, would have been aware of other metaphorical uses of the word from the Old Testament, including 'beginning'. Paul's use of *kephalê* approximates in meaning to *archê*, hence a new, and more illuminating, interpretation of various Pauline passages becomes possible.

Bedale points out that the light thrown on Paul by this rendering of *kephalê* is most striking in 1 Corinthians 11.3–12; the woman derives her being from man – as Eve does from Adam in 11.3. Derivation from a source implies subordination: in this case the order is woman, who is from man, who is from Christ, who is from God. Authority is, of course, implied, but this is derived from relative priority, which is causal, and not temporal, in the order of being. So this is a reference to spiritual differentiation, not to status or capacities.

With such an understanding of the meaning of 'head' Ephesians 5.22–33 is done greater justice. The church is the Eve of the Second Adam; Christ is 'head' to the church, as is Adam to Eve, and the reference in 2 Corinthians 11.3 to the 'fall' of Eve shows that this is a line of thought familiar to Paul's own mind. This understanding of the word throws light on the present passage. Ephesians 5.23 states that the submission of a wife to her husband is grounded in the relationship of the church to Christ. This is emphasized in particular by the assertion that the church owes its origin to Christ, as 'saviour of the body'. The 'but' of 5.24 is not strongly adversative, but simply takes up again the writer's main theme, and so in this passage 'but as the church' reminds the readers that the church has been brought into being by Christ, in the same sense that Eve owed her origin to Adam.

The purpose of the linguistic point here is that the husband is not being held up as the 'master' or 'ruler' of the wife, but as the source of her being. There is therefore clear reference to Adam in the background of this passage, so it is hardly surprising that the 'marriage' text of Genesis 2.24 is added. We shall look at this again in a moment.

A third reason for regarding the Ephesian 'household code' as a deliberate redaction of that in Colossians is that only the husband is given further instructions about correct behaviour; he is told how to love, but the wife is told neither how to submit, nor what her submission means theologically. This is surprising, in view of the ethical context of this section, which is entirely concerned with appropriate behaviour in the light of what is set out as the 'Pauline' gospel. In Colossians, on the other hand, the weight of the commands is balanced (even if the wife's relationship is subservient): the wife must submit as is fitting in the Lord, and the husband must 'love' and not be harsh.

Given the overall concern of the writer of Ephesians to work out, within the continuing Pauline tradition, a theological understanding which takes account of a changed situation, the exhortation to husbands to take as their pattern the love of Christ for the church cannot be without significance. The writer has a particular understanding of the church, which was elaborated in Ephesians 2, and in Ephesians 5 he presents his particular understanding of the body of Christ. The church is comprised of Jew and Gentile, and it is brought into being by the sacrificial death of Christ on the cross. But, more particularly, this doctrine is set out in Ephesians 2 in the context of the writer's desire to establish the unity between all people: for the writer of this epistle, it is a fact, both of Christian experience, and of apostolic gospel truth, that both Jews and Gentiles are members of the church; therefore the body of Christ includes the two races.

It is not unreasonable, consequently, to suppose that a similar understanding of the sacrifice of Christ is in the background of what the writer says in his exhortation to husbands to love their wives; the body of Christ includes both man and woman. This is developed in the exhortations which follow.

Hence the fourth point, which is that Christ's love is a submissive kind of love. Sampley (1971: 116) maintains that 'the husbands are nowhere in 5.22–33 exhorted to submission or anything like submission', and it is true that this is not demanded of them in explicit terms, in that the verb is not used. However, closer reflection upon the passage indicates a subtle development of the thought of Colossians; the whole meditation upon the love of Christ is an exhortation to submissive love.

The immediate exhortation is that husbands should love their wives just as Christ loved the church and 'gave himself for her'. This is a clear reference to the death of Christ as the sacrifice by which the church was brought into being, and it involved Christ's 'giving' of himself, and his consequent submission to death. No word such as 'submit' is used, it is true, but the idea of a costly self-surrender is none the less present, as may be seen in the expression '[he] gave himself for her' (5.25). The allusion to sacrifice is clear, as is also the reference to an atoning sacrifice made on behalf of the readers. With this may be compared Paul's language in Galatians 1.4, 'for our sins'; Galatians 2.20, 'for me'; and Galatians 3.13, 'a curse for us'.

The effects of this sacrifice are sanctification and cleansing. Abbott (1897: 168) notes that the 'ceremonial' idea of 'sanctify' appears to be the prominent one here, and the reference is presumably to those sacrifices in Jewish religion by which such sanctification and cleansing were brought about. 'Sanctification' is what is effected in the sacrificial liturgy of Israel by the offering, or 'presenting', of sacrificial animals. Here no animals are offered, for Christ offered his own body.

The washing of water mentioned in 5.26 is a reference to baptism, according to most commentators. However, Stevenson (1982: 11) refers, a little more convincingly, to the Jewish practice of a ceremonial washing of the bride before the betrothal rite. He observes that the distinction between betrothal and marriage may be reflected in that between redemption and consummation in this passage. In the clause 'in order that he might present to himself a glorious church', the verb used is the same as that which Paul uses in 2 Corinthians 11.2 to refer to his own metaphorical presentation of the Corinthian church as bride to Christ the bridegroom. The reference there would appear to be to betrothal, so this could refer either to betrothal or to marriage.

If there is a reference to baptism in Ephesians 5.26, it is brought to the service of a composite image comprising both sacrifice and betrothal, or marriage. If this is the case, then the 'word' by which the cleansing is effected could be either the gospel which is preached prior to baptism, or some such formula of baptism as 'in the name of the Father and of the Son, and of the Holy Spirit', which John Chrysostom favoured, or, perhaps, the name of Jesus. In this particular case, however, the 'word' is most likely to be the words of promise, or of contract, in the betrothal rite. This is regarded as a covenant in Malachi 2.14, and, according to Stevenson (1982: 4–5), it included an agreement to marry.

In all of these cases, it is clear that the writer is dealing with the imagery of ceremonies rather than with that of relationships, and this is of particular significance for the sacrificial imagery which follows.

This leads naturally to the fifth point, that in this section, the marriage *relationship* between husband and wife is seen as the wedding *ceremony* between Christ and the church. The 'ceremony' is the sacrifice of Christ upon the cross, which brought about the church's existence; for Christ is the Saviour of the body, and salvation, for the writer of Ephesians, is the work of grace, known by faith (Ephesians 2.8). It is this which reveals the love of Christ. As has already been observed, the clause, 'in order that he might present to himself a glorious church', suggests betrothal or marriage. Most commentators – for example Abbott (1897: 169), Barth (1974: 627–9), Robinson (1904: 207–8), Schlier (1963) – tend to rule out, or simply not consider, the idea of the presentation of a sacrificial offering. Yet in view of the later description of the church, in its glorified state, as 'without spot, wrinkle or any such thing', which is obviously sacrificial terminology, one wonders whether this rejection is a little hasty. Certainly, a 'spot' could be a simple mark on the body diminishing the beauty of the bride, just as a 'blemish' could. However, when the two words are brought together, with the intention that the offering be 'holy and blameless', it is difficult to avoid the conclusion that some idea of sacrifice is intended. To whom this is offered is not said, though it must, presumably, be to God.

Young (1982) makes the significant point that the whole idea of sacrifice so pervaded the culture of New Testament times that almost any religious ceremony might be regarded as a sacrifice. So here, 'sacrifice' terminology brings together various understandings of the relationship of Christ to his body, whether as bride or as sacrifice. Clearly, there is here no unambiguous parallel between the Christ/church and the husband/wife relationships, but, as has already been said, the two images are mingled for a total theological – and ethical – effect which is full of ambiguity, and which, the writer himself later confesses, is a great mystery.

The church is presented 'without spot, wrinkle or any such thing' in so far as it is a kind of offering. But the church is not the sacrifice. Christ cleaves to his *sacrificial* body in death, in order to save – that is, bring into being – his *glorious* body, the church. The contours have thus become unclear between the physical body of the Christ who died, and the resurrected body, which is the object of Christ's love, which is the church. This will be discussed later.

The purpose of this elaboration of the sacrifice of Christ is precisely to show that Christ's is what might be called a submissive love, involving the giving of himself. The bride is honoured in the act of Christ's sacrifice, as the recipient of his sacrificial love; she is not simply relegated to a position of subservience. The idea of Christ's presenting his body as a sacrifice (to God) is brought together with the idea of his presenting his bride to himself in marriage or betrothal – with ritual or ceremonial undertones, as the words of Genesis 2.23 imply, 'This is flesh of my flesh.'

The body which Christ offered was clearly his own physical body, and the writer of the Epistle to the Ephesians needs now to make the obvious statement that a man normally cares for his own body, and ought to love his wife in the same way. This image of the nuptial ceremony between Christ and the church sheds light on the marriage relationship. He who loves his wife loves his own self, which is his own physical body. The husband is called upon to act in the sphere of daily behaviour as Christ acted in the sphere of God's eternal plan, which is understood ceremonially.

Thus the man's love for his wife is to be as for his own body, and this is spelt out as involving the meeting of its demands for nourishment and cherishing. It is possible, however, that the statement 'for no one yet hated his own body, but nourishes and cherishes it, just as Christ [does] with the church' is made, not only because it spells out the practical ways in which a husband should show his love for his wife, but also because it deals with a very real difficulty which arises out of the setting together of the nuptial and the sacrificial images.

The difficulty is that the two images conflict: (a) the church is Christ's body; (b) the church is Christ's bride. Christ offered his body in death, and yet this death brought about the bride's existence. In other words, with the nuptial metaphor, Christ and his body, the church, are brought together in the ceremony, whereas with the sacrificial image, Christ, inseparable from his body, makes an offering of it. The body that marries the bride is sacrificed. The fusion of the two images might lead to the confusing idea that Christ makes a sacrifice of the church. Thus one might be tempted to ask, is the bride the sacrifice? The answer is, No, for no one would treat a bride in such a way; the idea is excluded by the writer's insistence on provision and care – nourishment and cherishing – just as Christ cared and provided for his bride, the church.

The further example is given of the kind of love which the husband is to exercise towards his wife, though the reason given – 'for we are members of his body' – raises again the problem of the fused images. These are brought together by means of Genesis 2.24, which, as the writer himself confesses, is a great mystery.

The quotation from Genesis is thus the scriptural passage which clinches the argument about mutuality by resolving the difficulty of the fusion of images: nuptial and sacrificial imagery can be accommodated by an image which embraces the two, and that is the image of 'one flesh'. Genesis 2.24 provides evidence for the view that Christ and church are 'one flesh'. A man gives up his mother and father, cleaves to his wife, and they become 'one flesh'.

Christ gives up himself – Paul in Philippians 2.7 has him 'emptying himself' – and he becomes 'head' or 'source' for the church. Christ therefore 'submitted', and this provides the basis for the writer's exhortation to the husbands to love with a sacrificial kind of love which is akin to submission. The passage therefore underlines the mutuality of the submission demanded by the writer. This mystery is indeed great, and, as the writer says, it refers to Christ and the church.

Sampley (1971: 54) is of the opinion that the quotation from Genesis 2.24 indicates that the writer intends a position of passivity for the wife. 'At no point is the wife the subject of the action, instead she is the object.' Perhaps this may be so, but in this particular context the quotation is clearly used to underline what the writer has already taught about the nature of the love which the husband is called to show to the wife. This suggests that it is not so much the passivity of the wife which is important, but the submissive and sacrificial activity of the husband. As Sampley rightly notes, the reference to Genesis 2.24 recalls the image of Adam and Eve's as the prototypical marriage; there is, as he says, a sense in which the marriage of Christ and the church supplants it. Adam imagery for Christ here is supplemented by Eve imagery for the church.

The 'mystery' is thus to be seen in the context of the use of this word elsewhere in Ephesians: both in 1.9, where its content is the 'summing up' of all things in Christ; and in 3.3, where Paul is revered as the apostle *par excellence* for his insight into the nature of the gospel. It is not only the mystery of marriage; nor does it only express the writer's wonder at how marriage, the formation of the church and the church's intimate relationship with Christ are brought together; it also takes on something of the signifi cance of the mystery of the Pauline gospel of the 'summing up of all things'.

At this stage the text reaches the limit of what can be said, so the readers are left with a call for the church to worship Christ – and for wives to revere their husbands precisely because the husbands are exhorted to imitate this Christ-like, sacrificial self-giving. The use of the term 'fear' echoes the 'numinous' note sounded in the idea of the 'mystery'. It also takes seriously the 'in the fear' of Ephesians 5.21, which was changed from 'in the Lord' in Colossians 3.18 because the writer wished to make a specifically christological point here. A religious awe is thus regarded as the appropriate response to the love of Christ in making his sacrifice in order to bring the church into being by the act of betrothal. The bride expresses a sense of wonder, or 'fear' at this submissive love, and the word, along with its cognate here, expresses this sense of awe.

As far as behaviour is concerned, for the writer of Ephesians, it is taken for granted that the wife will submit. What is new is that the husband will also submit, and so evoke the wonder of the wife. In order to evoke this appropriate response in the wife, the husband is to demonstrate a sacrificial and self-giving love.

MARRIAGE IMAGERY

It will be useful to set out the cultural and theological background to this marriage imagery in Ephesians. Schlier (1963: 264) provides a lengthy discursus on the *hieros gamos*, or 'sacred marriage', in the literature of the hellenistic world. He argues there that the attempt to explain the marriage imagery by reference to Old Testament texts – such as Hosea 1–3; Isaiah 49.18, 50.1ff., 54.1, 61.10, 62.4f.; Jeremiah 2.2; Ezekiel 16.1ff., 32.1ff. – is insufficient, because these are all simply metaphors in which Israel's relationship with Yahweh is compared with a marriage or a wedding. Schlier points out that these passages are never quoted in the Pauline writings (he ascribes Ephesians to Paul). Such passages cannot have formed the background to what Paul and the writer to the Ephesians say. Neither, says Schlier, can Jewish or Rabbinic ideas be sufficient for the origin of the Pauline idea. The Messiah is never called the bridegroom, and there is no reference to the idea of a marriage between the Messiah and Israel.

Schlier examines a number of New Testament passages which go a certain way to providing the necessary background, but which he dismisses as insufficient as a basis for doing so. Among the New Testament writings other than those of Paul, he makes three distinctions:

1 John 3.29 is a metaphor and not an allegory;
2 The comparison which is made in the synoptic Gospels – especially in Mark 2.18ff.; Matthew 22.1ff., 25.1ff. – is not between Messianic-time and marriage, but rather between Messiah and bridegroom, and the disciples are either the guests or the girl attendants, and not the bride;
3 It is not until Revelation 19.7, 21.2,9, 22.17 that any explicit

comparison is made between the exalted and returning Christ as the bridegroom and the present and future church with the bride. The Lamb, and the new Jerusalem which descends from heaven, are the bridal pair. In fact, Schlier maintains, it is only the Book of Revelation that comes anywhere near to saying what is said in Ephesians 5.22, and there is no reference there to the Redeemer as the bridegroom, nor of the marriage as a saving event. Marriage is seen purely eschatologically; the believers of the present are the invited guests.

Schlier then considers the possibility that 2 Corinthians 11.2 underlies Ephesians 5.22. The apostle 'betrothed' the disciples to Christ, and the marriage takes place at the parousia; till then he wishes to keep them pure and chaste. Schlier says that, after 2 Corinthians 11.3, without further explanation, Paul compares the church with Eve, who was deceived by the snake, noting that Genesis 1–3 played an important role in Jewish haggadah (cf. 1 Timothy 2.13, where the creation of Adam and Eve and the seduction of Eve are brought together). Thus 2 Corinthians 11.2 and Ephesians 5.22ff. are concerned not only with church/bride imagery, but also the context of these ideas with the exegesis of particular passages in Genesis 1–3.

However, Schlier continues, certain differences must be recognized. 2 Corinthians is written for a local community, whereas Ephesians 5.22 is for the whole church. More importantly, in Ephesians Christ presents the bride, but in 2 Corinthians the apostle does. The most significant fact, however, is that the whole bridal/marriage imagery is set within a context of the giving, cleansing, presenting, union and care of the church by Christ, and that within the context of saving events. Also, the imagery is used as the basis and ideal of earthly marriage, which finds its fulfilment in it. This idea is not present in the Old Testament, nor in any Jewish antecedents, nor in any existing contemporary material.

Schlier therefore turns to an explanation of the *hieros gamos* on the basis of Greek mythology, including Zeus and Hera; ritual holy marriage in Samothrace from the second century BC; Adonis in Alexandria; the reference in Pausanias II.11.3 to Demeter, Persephone and Iacchos; the marriage of Cadmus and Harmonia. However, none of these have any reference to the idea that earthly marriage should be modelled upon that of the gods – except perhaps in the story of Dionysos and Ariadne.

The idea of the *hieros gamos* came into Judaism via Philo, *de Abrahamo* 99f., concerning the marriage of mind and virtue. This marriage led to the birth of virtues. The Wisdom of Solomon (8.2,9,16,17; 9.4; 10.1) also has an idea of the *hieros gamos*. There is thus evidence of a pre-Christian myth in hellenistic circles, Schlier says, but this does not mean that a direct relationship with Paul can be shown; indeed, the relationship of Ephesians with Colossians shows this to be rather more complex.

However, Schlier (op. cit. 272) then goes on to argue that texts which are of a later date may also claim some influence on Ephesians, for they embody earlier traditions. He therefore argues for the presence of a Gnostic Sophia myth behind the marriage imagery here. He refers to the syzygy between heaven and earth in 2 Clement, and draws attention also to passages in the Shepherd of Hermas, the Didache, and both the Valentinian system and the Ophites as referred to by Irenaeus.

However, there is no need of the Sophia myth here. As has been shown, the sacrificial terminology may be understood on the basis of Jewish scriptures; indeed, this is all the more appropriate after the discontinuation of sacrifice at Jerusalem. The wall of partition has been broken down (according to Ephesians 2), and one new 'man', Christ's body, the church, has been created. Marriage imagery is used to depict the relationship of Christ and the church in such a way that partners in actual human marriages will learn mutually to submit to one another in order to express the self-giving love of God in Christ. At the same time, and conversely, the mutual submission of husband and wife is taken and used as an image of the relationship between Christ and his bride, the church.

THE WISE WALK

In Ephesians, the 'summing up' of all things takes on a number of meanings: it is the 'bringing to a conclusion'; it is the 'bringing back to the source', or renewing; it is also the consummation of all things. Here in this section, as throughout the ethical section of the epistle, the 'summing up' is enacted by the whole community. The basis for this enactment is in the context of the community's worship, and it is worked out in its life of thanksgiving, which involves the mutual submission of the community's members.

This is the case in the remaining exhortations in the household code. Fathers are addressed differently from those in Colossians:

neither are to provoke their children to wrath, but in Ephesians they are given an alternative; children are to be brought up in the 'discipline and instruction' of the Lord, whereas in Colossians the children simply must not become 'discouraged'. Similarly, masters are not simply to treat their slaves 'justly and fairly', because the masters also have a master in heaven; they are to have the same attitude as the slaves themselves, they are to 'forbear threatening', and they are to bear in mind that in God there is no 'respect of persons'. A kind of mutuality is asserted even here.

The presence of household codes in New Testament letters is a clear sign of the church settling down to social life, as Dibelius (1953) noted. The household code in Colossians provided an ideal opportunity for the author of Ephesians to develop his theology of 'summing up'. It was to be rooted in life as it was lived (especially after the destruction of Jerusalem in AD 70), and it was of theological substance, thanks to the applicability of Genesis 2.24, 'for this reason a man shall leave his father and mother and cleave to his wife, and the two shall become one flesh'. It was therefore also capable of theological reflection and development. The 'care' in Ephesians 5.15 which is to be exercised by the believers in their 'worthy walk' involves the necessary recognition and practice of mutuality within the community.

The Epistle to the Ephesians continues Pauline tradition. The marriage imagery in the epistle is a case of remarkable creativity which sets out an understanding of the marital relationship as the nuptial ceremony between Christ and the church. This makes possible a new understanding of the relationship between husband and wife, one of mutual submission, which is the way of life appropriate for those who have been incorporated by baptism into Christ's one body, the church, through his sacrificial death on the cross. Christ's 'sacrificial' offering, now newly understood, is of his own body ('flesh of my flesh') offered not to God, as bloody sacrifice, but to himself, as celestial bride.

The event which brought the church into being is also that which effected, in principle, the 'summing up' of all things, and in which the community's members are invited – and expected – to participate, by walking worthy of this calling. This walk, or manner of life, is not like that of Gentiles, which formerly they were. It is a walk in love, in the light, undertaken with great care, because the days are evil. Moreover, the walk continues until the powers are finally defeated, and the consummation is finally brought about.

The Ephesian household code thus introduces the image of mutual submission to one another, in order to stress, again, that the work of God, the 'summing up' of all things in Christ, continues in and through the life of his body, the church.

Chapter 8

The armour of God

The final section of the epistle, 6.10–24, constitutes the climax and conclusion, both to the ethical section of the epistle which begins in 4.1, and to the epistle as a whole. The text takes further the insight which Paul was granted into the content of the gospel, which was expressed in the Benediction in terms of God's plan to 'sum up' all things in Christ. In the course of the Thanksgiving the implications of this were set out as they affect 'things in the heavenlies' and 'things on the earth'. After a recollection of the significance of Paul in the divine scheme of things, the ethical section explained the way of life, or 'walk', which is the appropriate response to God's saving acts. In this final section the readers are urged to put on God's armour, in order to be able to defend themselves against attacks from the forces of evil. The armour is itemized, to some extent, and the readers are urged to give themselves to prayer for the apostle's ministry. In the light of the rest of the epistle, it is reasonable to suppose that the themes of unity, mutuality and reconciliation are present as leitmotifs. Since the emphasis throughout the epistle has been corporate and liturgical, it would be surprising if this were not continued to the end.

Most commentators interpret the section as though the image of the soldier refers to the individual Christian. However, in view of the thrust of the argument throughout the whole epistle, it is better understood as referring to the church as a whole. The argument for this interpretation may be set out under the following headings.

THE INTRODUCTION TO THE MILITARY IMAGERY

Underlying this section is the conviction that Christ is victorious over all the evil powers of the cosmos; this victory has already been referred to in 1.20–3, in that Christ has been given a position of superiority over the powers. In 1.20–3 it is made quite clear that it is the victory on earth which has brought about the victory in heaven, and the readers are already said in 2.6 to have their existence 'in the heavenly realm'. The powers, over which the decisive battle has already been won, have yet to submit to its verdict; though dead, they will not lie down, but still wage war against the body of Christ. The victory consisted in the resurrection of Christ and the consequent bringing into being of the church, which is Christ's resurrected body. That body is depicted in this passage in a particular image; and the writer made clear that the consummation of all things comes about in and through the defeat of the forces of evil in all the attacks which they institute against the risen Christ and his body.

The church, in its turn, is called upon to share in that victory by taking up weapons in the battle. The struggle is inevitable, since it is a defence against attacks made by an assailant. The act of defence is therefore not one option among others for the believers; there is no alternative but to take up arms against the attack of the evil one and the forces at his disposal. However, because the armour and the weaponry are God's own, the exhortation is to be read as much as an encouragement as a command. The writer introduces the final section of the epistle with the word 'finally', and the readers are urged to 'be strong in the Lord and in his powerful strength'. The power which strengthens believers is the power they receive as a gift from God. The words for 'strength' are used synonymously, and any distinctions between them are too forced; the overall effect is achieved by the repetition of synonyms.

The expression 'in the Lord' (Schlier 1963: 289) shows both where the strength comes from and what it is. It is God's power at work in the believers (cf. 1.19, 3.20). In 3.16 the apostle is seen to pray that the readers will increase in God's power, and this power is that which is displayed in the resurrection. The exhortation which introduces the image of the armour of God thus highlights two significant points about the passage. First, the power in which the battle is fought is that of God, the Lord, himself – and one wonders whether 'the Lord' is to be understood also as Christ, in what is therefore a studied christological ambiguity here. Second, and consequently, that power cannot be defeated; the genitival construction of the phrase, if it has any semantic substance above the purely stylistic (indicating something like 'mighty power'), is evidence of this. Adequate defence is therefore guaranteed to those who share the Lord's strength. Third, the writer associates the believers most closely with the experience of the resurrection.

In 6.11 the armour of God is introduced with the words, 'Put on the whole armour of God, that you may be able to stand against the wiles of the devil.' The armour is not simply that which God supplies, but also which is God's very own. Clearly, the battle is God's battle, so the equipment for it cannot be merely human defence. The image provided here (Barth 1974: 787) may be that of a Roman foot soldier, although Jewish armour was essentially the same. Polybius (*Historia* 6.23) lists Roman armour as consisting of shield, sword, greaves, spear, breastplate and helmet. The spear is omitted here, but girdle and shoes are added. These, although not armour, were an essential part of a soldier's dress. The image of God's armour also occurs in Isaiah 59.17, Wisdom of Solomon 5.17ff., Ecclesiasticus 46.6 and *Ignatius to Polycarp* 6. However here the image is both more sustained and also developed to a far greater degree than the metaphors elsewhere in the Hebrew Bible.

The reason for putting on the armour here is so that the readers may be able to stand against the 'wiles of the devil'. They are not expected to engage in offensive warfare, but to 'stand their ground' against attacks made upon them. The fact that the church is not called to be on the offensive is striking, and one might ask why this is so. Most probably, firstly, it is because the defeat of the powers has already occurred in the resurrection. Second, however, given the liturgical context of the epistle, it is perhaps possible that the idea of 'standing' for worship and for prayer is also present; it is as the community lives specifically in the context of its worship that its defence is endured; as we shall see, much is made at the end of the passage (6.18–20) of the value of the community's praying. The noun 'devil' is also used in 4.27. Here he employs 'wiles': the word suggests not only deceit, but also cunning. Caird prefers 'stratagems' rather than 'wiles': 'the required combination of tactical shrewdness and ingenious deception' (1976: 92).

The idea of Christian warfare is also present in 2 Corinthians 10.3ff. and 2 Timothy 2.3, and the theme of warfare is a recurrent one in Old Testament pictures of God's dealings with his enemies. Houlden (1977: 339) draws attention to the familiar title 'Lord of hosts', or 'armies', which goes back to Israel's earliest days. He observes that it is also a commonplace in religion to see deities as warriors, and their followers as soldiers in their armies. The image would have been heightened for first-century readers by the revolt of the Maccabees in the second century BC. In the writings of the Qumran sect, the War Scroll indicates its importance for the final battle between God and his enemies. The writer is at pains to point out that the battle is not, however, an earthly, human one: 'for we wrestle not against blood and flesh, but against principalities, against the powers, against the world rulers of this present darkness, against the spiritual hosts of wickedness in the heavenly places' (Ephesians 6.12). The order 'blood and flesh' is striking, since this pair of words is usually found in the reverse order.

Abbott (1897: 181) maintains that the words 'principalities' and 'powers' cannot be understood apart from the parallel use of them in Colossians 1.16. However, in Colossians Paul is contending against a doctrine of angelic mediators, whereas here the writer is alluding to a distinctive, though closely related, understanding of created spiritual beings. Some scholars have speculated on the existence of ranks of angelic mediators. The *Testament of Levi* 3 has seven orders; Origen refers to five classes; Ephraem of Syria to three, and Pseudo-Dionysius (in *On the Celestial Hierarchy*) to three. However, such speculation is set aside by the assertion of Christ's supremacy over all. Earthly powers are referred to as principalities and powers in Titus 3.1, and they are clearly regarded as evil in Ephesians 6.12.

Abbott (1897: 181f.) gives careful consideration to 'world rulers' in this verse. He notes that the term is used in classical writers and (transliterated) in Rabbinic traditions. It is also used of the four kings whom Abraham pursued, in order to add glory to Abraham's victory. The angel of death is called *kosmokrator*, 'world ruler', and the word is also used in the *Testaments of the Twelve Patriarchs*. The word was certainly popular among the Valentinian Gnostics of the following century; according to Irenaeus, Gnostics referred to the devil in this way. Abbott refers to a view that Rabbis and Jews are intended here, on the basis of a passage in the Talmud where Rabbis are to be regarded as kings (cf. the possible use of such a concept in Acts 4.26). But the context here demands a meaning within the spiritual sphere (cf. the designation of Satan as 'the God of this present age' in 2 Corinthians 4.4, and 'the ruler of this world' in John 14.30).

Because the enemy which attacks the church is none other than the enemy of God himself, the armour to be put on must be that which God himself wears in his fight with the forces of evil. Only this will enable the Christians to 'stand in at the evil day' and still be standing when the battle is over – which is presumably how the phrase 'and having done all, to stand', is to be understood. The 'evil day' is the apocalyptic battle, according to Schlier. Fischer (1973: 166) agrees, but says this was lost in the dualism of the broader hellenistic environment. When that day is over, the worship of God will be the sole object of the existence of the people of God.

INDIVIDUALIST READINGS

It is a curious phenomenon of the history of the exegesis of this epistle that apparently all its interpreters have assumed that the image in 6.10–20 is to be interpreted as referring to the individual Christian, perceived as a soldier. This tradition in exegesis goes back to the earliest times, and there are a number of reasons why interpreters have persistently understood the text in this way.

Few commentators have considered the importance of the context of this section within the overall structure of the epistle as a whole. It follows the section of household codes, and the specific adaption of the last of them to an exhortation about mutuality in the marriage relationship. Traditional exegesis of that passage, however, has failed to note the emphasis on mutuality, and so it is perhaps hardly surprising that this passage which follows should also be understood so individualistically. Typically, commentators tend to talk about a final exhortation to Christians to 'stand firm'.

Nor have commentators noted the liturgical nature of the epistle, which was elaborated in chapter 1 above (see pp. 11–14). Any interpretation of the epistle needs to take seriously the atmosphere of worship generated by the Benediction, the tone of the Thanksgiving, the frequent prayers and the pleonastic language of the epistle as a whole. This tendency to individualism in exegesis is perhaps understandable in the light of the practice of minute, detailed study of the text by scholars in private. If early preachers were as concerned as their modern counterparts to apply the text first to themselves and then to their congregations, it is not difficult to see how the individual might come to figure more than the community.

It is also clear that concentration on the details of the armour, rather than on the theological substance of the imagery, has led to an undue emphasis on the image itself; and since the image is, after all, of a soldier, an individual comes naturally to mind. This is particularly true of the interpretations of Abbott and Barth, who both go to some lengths to itemize the articles of equipment and weaponry.

Gnostic accounts of the background to the imagery here also tend towards an individualistic exegesis, since Gnosticism was essentially a religion of individual salvation. However, it is becoming increasingly clear that the Gnosticism made use of Ephesians, rather than the other way round. Gnosticism was essentially an individual, private kind of religion, and in supposing its influence here, these scholars have also assumed its individualism.

Finally, as a result of a lack of understanding of the fact and the psychology of pseudepigraphy, commentators have too easily referred to those passages in the uncontested writings of St Paul, and to the later epistles to Timothy and Titus, where images of warfare, weaponry and virility are used to exhort Christians to firmer belief and action. However, as it has been the intention of this *Reading* to make clear, Ephesians was written by a Pauline disciple, who wanted in particular to emphasize the apostle's teaching about the reconciliation, unity and mutuality of love and service within the church.

The early history of the exegesis of this passage is typified by that of John Chrysostom, who interpreted the image as applying to individuals, and referred constantly to the command laid on every Christian to stand and do battle with evil (Migne, PG xx: 163ff.), and this would accord with the Fathers' concern to show how the scriptures taught true doctrine. This tradition of exegesis continues with other early Fathers and throughout the Middle Ages. (For other patristic and medieval exegesis of Ephesians, see the bibliography in Schlier 1963.) It is therefore hardly surprising – even if perhaps still a little disappointing – that more modern scholars pursue the same line of exegesis.

Abbott (1897: 180–90) does not make it explicit, but the tone of his commentary on these verses is quite unambiguous: the soldier is an image of the individual Christian. Robinson notes (1904: 133) that the battle between God and the forces of evil has already been won, but that the triumph must now be realized in the church; however he does not develop, in his subsequent commentary on the text, an understanding of the church in this passage. In his introductory analysis of the epistle he entitles this section 'The spiritual warrior clad in God's armour', which suggests that he also understood the passage in an individual sense.

More recently, Schlier (1963: 229) speaks of 'the Christians', in the plural, but does not appear to understand them to be addressed corporately as the church. Fischer says quite clearly that the reference is individual: 'The context of the meaning of the individual weapons is no longer the final eschatological battle, but the common situation of the Christian. . . . The next question is . . . how this understanding of God's weaponry and its transfer to the individual Christian has arisen' (1973: 166).

Barth makes the quite specific point that in Ephesians 'the Qumranite concern with proper ranks and tactics is replaced by the confidence that God will give his weapons to each one of the saints and that this armour will suffice for all their needs' (1974: 792). He does, however, claim that the emphasis of these verses is the 'special concern' of Ephesians, which is 'to present the gospel as a message related to man's social essence and existence'. But he says this simply to contradict the interpretation of the passage which would see it as aimed at the internal struggles of individual Christians against their own passions – as in the interpretation of St Jerome – and not in order to highlight the essentially corporate nature of the image of the armour.

Caird (1976: 91) entitles his commentary on this section 'The Christian Soldier', and refers to his temptations, his equipment, the need for him to stand his ground and trust his armour, and the importance of his watch in prayer; thus he too fails to note any corporate meaning in the passage.

Houlden (1977: 337–40) talks consistently of the individual Christian believer, noting that some scholars see the whole passage as addressed specifically to those recently baptized. In particular he sees the Christian as the 'bringer of release, salvation, such as he already enjoys' to those who are under the enslaving power of evil. The armour of God enables him to do this. There is no corporate reference at all.

Finally, Schnackenburg (1982: 34) also refers to 'the Christian's struggle against the forces of evil'. The tone of his commentary on this passage is individualist, and he does not seem to be aware of the possibility of a more corporate view.

However, to restate the argument, an altogether different emphasis is being made in this epistle, which is not to urge individual Christians to grow in the faith, but to encourage the whole church, as a body, to see the historical vindication of St Paul, and to grow into the renewed and reconciled Man which is the risen Christ. The liturgical presupposition is of primary importance here; the worshipping community is regarded by the writer of Ephesians as the complete man who stands before God.

A CORPORATE UNDERSTANDING

Now that an attempt has been made to understand the dominance of what might be called 'individualist' exegesis, the elaboration of an alternative, corporate interpretation is called for.

The first reason why a corporate understanding is more appropriate is that both the structure of the whole epistle and the grammar and syntax of this passage seem to prefer it. The observation has been made earlier that Ephesians is a 'liturgical letter' (p. 68; see also pp. 18–25 above), that is, a communication addressed to a community, with the intention that it be read aloud at worship. It therefore contains ascriptions of praise to God, passages of theological reflection and important sections of ethical teaching. The whole of the epistle focuses upon the corporate nature of Christian origin, existence and behaviour. It is therefore most likely that the final section of the epistle should end with an emphasis not on the individual, but on the corporate nature of Christian being.

Furthermore, the context of the passage demands that the corporate image established in the household code, especially in what is said about the marriage relationship, be retained. The argument was pursued in the previous chapter that the writer goes to some lengths to underline his view that what is important about the marriage relationship is the mutuality of submission which is required by each of the partners to the other, following the example of Christ in his attitude to the church. It is in mutual submission that the essential unity of the church is brought to expression. The household code hints that the other relationships in the household – parents with children, masters with slaves – are also to retain this element of mutuality. It is natural, therefore, to understand the passage Ephesians 6.10ff. as having a similar thrust.

The second argument in favour of a corporate understanding arises from the present application of the insights of sociology and anthropology to the study of the New Testament, for in the light of these it is arguable that an individualist interpretation of the passage would not be in keeping with the self-understanding of a community in such a social context in that period of history. Malina (1983) has shown how people in first-century societies understood themselves as living primarily in relationship with one another as part of a group. The first-century person would consequently see himself through the eyes of other people. This meant that other people were needed for any sort of meaningful existence. Behaviour was based upon living up to what others thought, and the word 'conscience' – in Latin *conscientia*, and in Greek *suneidesis* – gives expression to the idea that it is 'knowledge along with others'; one might even use the expression 'common sense', though not in its modern everyday meaning, but rather in the sense of knowledge which is shared with other people, and which provides the key to living. 'A person with conscience is a respectable, reputable, and honourable person' (1983: 51).

Malina develops this idea into the concept of 'dyadic personality'. What counts in a culture where this concept predominates is the honour only of those whose opinion one values, such as Paul in 1 Corinthians 4.1–4, where he is concerned only about the Corinthians' estimate of him. The question of a personal sense of individual guilt does not arise. This is due to the fact that the first-century person was not interested in personality and psychology, in our modern senses; the 'individual' was understood differently, for people saw themselves in terms of the 'significant other'. Honour and shame, rather than guilt, were pivotal values. The questions which perplex us about our life today tend to be answered by reference to inner motivation, personality and awareness of psychology. However, in New Testament times, those questions would have been approached upon the basis of 'dyadism'. Persons need other people to enable them to know who they are, and this highlights the importance of interpersonal behaviour in such societies. In questions of responsibility for morality and deviance, the individual was not the main concern.

It would, of course, be possible on this basis to argue that, in Ephesians, it is still the individuals who are addressed, though in a context which is to be understood in the terms which have just been elaborated. However, the considerations which Malina raises alter the whole emphasis in reading. This is especially so in the case of the theological terms which follow, namely truth, righteousness and readiness to preach. These terms characterize the whole community, or the relationships within it, rather than the virtues of its members. There is an analogy with the passage in 2.21–2, where reference is made to the importance of the 'joints' which are 'supplied' to a building in order to enable to grow into 'a holy temple'.

Malina then goes on to talk about 'zoning', which is a most revealing concept when applied to the image of the armour. 'Zones' are areas of the body which affect the aspects of life and feeling. He points out that the specific understanding of dyadic personality differed from culture to culture. The Greeks and Romans thought in terms of body and soul; intellect, will and conscience; virtues and vices. Semitic thinking, however, was not so introspective; the emphasis was rather on externally perceptible activity and the social functions of such activity. The make-up of the individual was perceived metaphorically as a human organism, with a heart for thinking and eyes for receiving data; with a mouth for speaking and ears for collecting the speech of others; and with hands and feet for acting.

Malina argues that there were 'three mutually interpenetrating yet distinguishing zones of interacting with environments': the zone of emotion-fused thought, the zone of self-expressive speech and the zone of purposeful action. These zones were brought together in the totality of the person, in that inmost reactions (eyes and heart) were expressed in language (mouth and ears) or outwardly realized in activity (hands and feet). The three zones comprise the non-introspective make-up of a man and are used to describe human behaviour throughout the Bible. Significantly, for our purposes here, Malina goes on to say, 'When all three zones are mentioned, the writer is alluding to total and complete human experience' (1983: 62).

If these 'zones' are applied to the image of the armour in this passage, it is interesting to note that the armour might be divided thus:

girded loins	activity
breastplate (of righteousness)	activity
footwear (for preaching the gospel)	language
shield (of faith)	inmost reaction
helmet (of salvation)	inmost reaction
sword (of the Spirit, word of God)	language

The application of Malina's analysis would suggest a total understanding of the organism, and suggest the image of a corporate man who is complete, integrated and at one, both with his environment and with himself. This would fit in very well with the image of the 'perfect man' which is an important key to understanding this passage.

The third argument in favour of a corporate view, as has just been hinted, is that an analysis of the theological terms in this section makes more sense in the light of a corporate understanding. None of the theological terms which underlie the military images may properly be said to be the property of individual believers, for they are all based upon either relationships within the community, or the community's shared knowledge of God through the gospel. They have their origin in God, and are either communicated to the church, or are marks of the church's life. In some respects they are characteristics of God, or Christ, and consequently of Christ's body, the church; thus only in a secondary sense are they marks of the individual believer.

The soldier is to stand with his 'loins girt about with truth' (6.14). The word 'truth' is used in Ephesians 1.13; 4.21,24,25; and 5.9, and the participle derived from it, 'truthing it', in 4.15. Truth of itself can hardly be a moral virtue, so it is clearly more appropriate in this context to understand it as the truth of the gospel. The community is thus urged to 'put on truth' in order to give bodily expression to the gospel. Abbott (1897: 185) disputes that this can be a reference to the truth of the gospel here, because it does not occur in the passage until later. But what comes later is a reference to the preaching of the gospel – 'evangelizing'. Truth is thus not primarily a private virtue, for the truth of the gospel is a foundational element in the community's life. This is therefore not an appeal to individuals to act faithfully – that has already been made in the ethical section in 4.15 – but one to the church, to recognize its origin in the 'truth' of Christ. Certainly, the readers are encouraged to show it in their corporate life, but the basis upon which this exhortation is made is the prior truth of the gospel.

The next item of the armour is 'righteousness' (6.14), and the same point may be made of that. The word also occurs in in 4.24 and 5.9. What is meant here is either to be understood merely as 'righteousness', 'uprightness' or 'rectitude' as a moral virtue, or there may be an element of the Pauline understanding of 'justi-fication'. It is unwise to draw too hard and fast a distinction between the ethical and the declaratory, however; justification, along with uprightness and moral rectitude, are received by faith. Barth (1974: 767–8) argues that neither 'truth' nor 'righteousness' in this context can be restricted to the moral sense. Ziesler (1972: 164–8) looks at the corporate dimension, but fails to develop it, and the tendency is certainly widespread to interpret this concept in Paul individualistically, but there are strong grounds for thinking that 'righteousness' is also primarily a corporate concept, for it refers to the status of believers in Christ who, *as a body*, have died to sin and are alive to righteousness in the cross and resurrection, made real to the church in baptism (Romans 6). Baptism is not a private ritual, but a public demonstration of the church's faith in the saving act of Christ. Whether or not the writer intends a particular Pauline sense of 'righteousness by faith' in the term here, the presence of both the Pauline background and the liturgical context suggests that more than a simple virtue is being referred to. Righteousness is an important personal virtue to the Hebrew mind, and the writer is saying that it should therefore be characteristic of the church, just as the other virtues which are related to the gospel proclamation.

Justification and righteousness together have a corporate dimension, for the idea is grounded in the resurrection of Jesus, in which his body was glorified when he was 'raised for (our) justification' (Romans 4.25). Baptism is the corporate experience by which all participate in the body; all are therefore justified. This justification is imparted, then, firstly from God to Christ, then to the church, and to the believer in so far as he or she participates in the body. The individual believer is certainly justified, but on the basis of the community's justification, and that by faith, which is also a characteristic of the community. Righteousness as a virtue also characterizes what we would call relationships, not individuals; 'righteous dealings' are therefore what are at issue here.

The church's feet are to be appropriately 'shod' (6.15). The footwear of soldiers recalls the Roman *caligae*, but for Ephesians this is for 'the preparation of the gospel of peace'. The word 'preparation' occurs only here in the New Testament. The word 'gospel' is found in Ephesians 1.13; 3.6; 6.15,19; 'peace' in Ephesians 1.2; 2.14,15,17; 4.3; 6.15,23. 'Peace' is that which is brought about by this preaching of Christ, according to the Pauline gospel as understood here in Ephesians. The gospel and the preaching of it is the church's task, and the church as a body must have a concern for spreading the good news of Jesus. It seems unlikely that individual Christians are being urged here to take to the road and preach the gospel, since this would be a question of gift, calling and authorization. The idea of feet being shod implies a practical readiness to take to the road, and perhaps recalls the passage in Isaiah 52.7, where the 'good news of peace' is that between God and Israel, which will allow the nation to return to the land. Here the church is to be characterized by the desire to preach the gospel, and the idea is that the church be characterized by a desire to continue Paul's mission to the world and a concern for peace. The context of Isaiah 52 is of the return, both of the people, and of God, and this image is also present in Isaiah 57, the passage which is used in Ephesians (see 2.11–22) to refer to the peace established between Jews and Gentiles. It is interesting to note that Abbott (1897: 185) says this is not a reference to a readiness to preach, since all Christians are addressed, but this objection is removed if the address is to the whole church.

The 'shield of faith' is the next item of equipment (6.16). Faith also occurs in Ephesians 1.15; 2.8; 3.12,17; 4.5,13; 6.23. This too is a mark of the community – in all of these cases. Faith is one, and it is the shared response to the grace of God in Christ. Certainly, Paul speaks of individuals having faith – most notably, Abraham in Romans 4, though the implications of that case of remarkable individuality are thoroughly corporate. Moreover, what is important in Ephesians is that faith characterizes the response of the Gentiles, as a race, to the gospel of Christ. Faith is therefore corporate in a sense prior to that in which it is individual.

The same may be said of 'salvation', for the soldier is to wear the 'helmet of salvation' (6.17). The precise word occurs only here in the Pauline corpus of letters, though a feminine form of it is found in Ephesians 1.3, and the cognate verb in Ephesians 2.5,6. As with the other characteristics, this is not a private possession. Salvation characterizes the action of God towards the Gentiles in Ephesians – and this is also a shared possession; salvation is 'sitting together' in the heavenlies in Ephesians 2.

The 'sword of the spirit' is the one item of weaponry mentioned. The word 'spirit' occurs in 1.13,17; 2.2,18,22; 3.5,16; 4.3,4,23,30; 5.18; 6.17,18. Again, the important point is that the Spirit resides in the believer by virtue of his primary residence in the church, which is the Temple of God (2.21–2). The sword is the Spirit, and it is not just given by the Spirit – the genitive is again one of apposition – and it is also the breath which bears the word of God, the 'word of God' of Ephesians 5.26. The word *logos* is used in Ephesians 1.13; 4.29; 5.6; 6.19, both of human words, and for the 'word of truth'.

Thus in spite of the strong tendency to see these as 'individual', following years of traditional interpretation, these highly theological virtues are not individual traits, but characteristics of God's dealing with the church, or they are based upon relationships within the community. They therefore characterize the community in a sense prior to that in which they characterize the individual believers within it.

The fourth argument in favour of a corporate understanding of the image of the armour of God is that greater clarity is given to the concept of the 'perfect man' in 4.13. The problem of the meaning of that term is clarified when it is recognized that this section is the conclusion to the ethical exhortation, as well as the climax to the whole letter, and when it is seen in the light of the virile, military image in Ephesians 6.10ff. Greater sense is also given to the idea of *teleios* as indicating completeness, or perfection, as an eschatological, or perhaps teleological, goal. The church is the 'perfect man', destined to grow into Christhood; he is therefore not the 'upright man' of James 3.2, but the eschatological figure of Christ as the second Adam in a renewed creation. The background to this is to be found, not in Gnosticism, as has been argued by some exegetes (see Barth 1974: 793), but in Jewish understandings of Adam, especially with regard to his height at creation, when he is said to have extended up to the heavens. Davies (1970: 45–6) refers to traditions concerning the height of Adam which may be traced back to Rabbinic writings of the end of the first century. In the light of this, Ephesians appears to be saying that the height of Adam before the Fall is regained at the consummation. One is reminded of the description of the risen Christ in the Gospel of Peter, where the height of the risen one presumably implies the same as the image here, the restoration of Adam. The 'perfect man' is thus a mythological figure to the modern reader because of the reference to Adam, but nevertheless, human, corporate and complete.

The fifth argument for a corporate view follows on from the fourth, and is that the plan of God to 'sum up all things in Christ' is further seen as involving the participation of the church's members. The 'summing up' is not only the ultimate and eternal design of the grace of God in which the church is invited to share, but also the goal to which the church is invited to contribute. 'Summing up' is therefore the eschatological, or teleological, creation of the 'perfect man'. This act of consummation involves six areas of meaning: summing up, crowning, completing, ruling, reconciling and starting again, or renewing.

These areas of meaning for the Greek term *anakephalaiôsis* come together in the course of the epistle, and they all have their primary fields of meaning in the context of that community which is the church. The summing up, derived from rhetoric, involves re-conciling, in the sense of bringing things together. This is a genuine reconciliation both between God and humanity and between the races of the world. The eschatological context of the action of God clearly also involves crowning, in the sense of bringing to an end; it also marks the completion of all things, in that things are brought to perfection. The renewal, or starting again, is that of the corporate Adam, and constitutes the rule of the corporate Christ over the forces of evil.

Finally, the liturgical setting of the epistle is emphasized, in that all these points make sense only as understood within the com-munity's worship and its offering of itself to God. The man seen here in armour is the community of Christians at worship, where, in the sight of God, battle is waged with the forces of evil.

SOME IMPLICATIONS OF THIS READING

The analysis of Ephesians 6.10–20 understood as a corporate image for the church at worship before God leads to a number of consequences, which are now set out.

Ephesians 6.10–20 is a fitting conclusion to the ethical material, for it completes the corporate and mutual tone of the ethics of the epistle. The metaphor changes from 'walk' in the ethical section, to 'stand' in this one. This is partly stylistic, but partly also a shift in emphasis which is as well called 'eschatological' as anything else, for there is an element of eschatology here. The image is of standing, not only in battle, but also before God, because the community stands in worship; and worship, just as the battle, is eschatological.

The section ends with what is clearly a central concern for the writer, namely that prayer should be offered for the furtherance of the apostle's mission. In view of the post-Pauline, pseudepigraphic nature of the epistle, this must be taken as a request for prayer that the Gentile mission might continue. The writer has clearly set out his belief that the church's life consists in the bringing together of Jew and Gentile in the one body of Christ. It has already been noted that prayer and worship are crucial to the understanding of Ephesians, even though this may be implicit rather than explicit, since the original context in which the epistle was read will have rendered unnecessary its clear statement. But prayer, worship and mission come together here.

Guiver (1993: 9) makes the point that Christian prayer was always primarily a corporate activity; personal prayer derives from the prayer of the church, which is prior. The theme of prayer is taken up immediately after the battle image of the sword of the Spirit, which is the word of God which the apostle preached. So in praying for the whole community of the church, the readers will be giving thanks to God for his grace shown in the gospel; and in praying particularly for the apostle, they will be taking a part in its further success. Their 'prayer' and 'supplication' are to take place 'at all times', which signifies the ceaselessness of the church's praying. It is also to be done 'in the Spirit', which, as is to be seen in other uses of the expression, is best understood as an instrumental use of the preposition: all praying is done with the Spirit's help.

The request is underlined, however, by the desire that, in order to pray, the readers remain watchful, alert and persevering; the church's prayers are to be on behalf of the church. In particular, however, there is to be intercession that Paul's ministry of preaching may be with boldness, so that the mystery of the gospel might be made known, for this is the whole purpose of the apostle's calling, as was made clear in Ephesians 3. There is thus an element of circularity here, in that prayer must continue to be offered, in order for Paul's mission to continue, in order that the spread of the gospel may flourish, in order that the divine plan for the 'summing up of all things' might be fulfilled and the church grow, in order that prayer may continue to be offered.

Ephesians 6.10–20 is therefore also a fitting conclusion to the whole epistle, since it portrays an image of a perfected church, reconciled and renewed, over which Christ rules as Lord; this is the 'summing up' of all things. The various linguistic and theological strands therefore come together in this final section. The powers are defeated, Jew and Gentile are reconciled, and consequently God and the whole of humanity are reconciled; the whole of the human community of the world is therefore recreated, or renewed, in the person of Christ, who is the perfect Man that Adam was destined to be. The church, the body of Christ, is the living embodiment of that re-creation and thus lives out in its own life, which is the microcosm of the whole creation, the rule of Christ, the reconciliation of all peoples and the new human order. The greeting which follows, in vv. 21–2, and which is dependent upon Colossians, provokes the comment that, in reworking that epistle, the writer of Ephesians has rendered more human the particularly 'cosmic' concern of Colossians.

In this passage, then, the 'summing up' is shown to be both christological and ethical – though neither to the exclusion of the other. However, it is 'ethical' in the broadest sense of the term – which has to do with the custom, usage, manners and habit of the Christian living in the church. The writer's concern is therefore not just for moral action, but that the whole of life should accord with the divine calling. That is the meaning of the worthy walk, and it involves, as has been shown above, a walk not like the life of the Gentiles, but a walk which is characterized by love, which is appropriate for children of light and which is 'careful', in the sense that it takes a realistic view of the needs of the other person, and is deliberate in its mutuality.

Worship is the context of the community's reflection. Houlden makes the point that the 'inspiring exhortation, so much more extended than anything in Paul's undoubted writings . . . helps to put Ephesians in the category of liturgy or oratory rather than epistle' (1977: 337). This prompts the observation that it is in worship that the 'hermeneutical gap' between the writing of the epistle and its reading in later ages may be bridged. The idea of the consummation of all things in the image of the perfect man, the corporate Christ, is present in hymnology, liturgy and prayer. Literal understandings do not play a large part in the imagination of worshippers, who operate with images. This brings us back, both to the centrality of worship for Christian existence, as it was so enthusiastically set out by Kavanagh, and to the insight into the nature of the liturgical letter. It is in worship – as the community stands before God, as it focuses upon the central theological themes of the gospel and as it sees itself as taking up arms for defence in the spiritual battle before the God who is the object of its worship – that the imagination of the people of God takes in both what is at present happening in the world, and what has happened both in and for the world in the saving grace of God as demonstrated in Jesus Christ.

The Epistle to the Ephesians is therefore a pertinent and imaginative reconstruction of the Pauline gospel for its own day, and in the light of its own community's needs. This suggests that there is therefore warrant in the very pages of scripture for readers and worshippers and believers in future ages to embark upon a similar course: the realizing of Paul's message in the setting and context of the church's worship, prayer and life in the world.

Postscript
'To sum up'

This *Reading* of the Epistle to the Ephesians has attempted a number of things. There are grounds for believing that the epistle was written by a Pauline disciple soon after the events of AD 70. This makes it an early pseudepigraph, which is consonant both with its evident pseudonymity, and with its attestation in the Fathers and presence in the earliest canonical lists; it was such an early creation that its precise origin was obscured by the time of the earliest lists of Christian scriptures.

The purpose of the epistle's writing was to vindicate the name of Paul as God's chosen instrument to bring the gospel to the Gentiles, especially in the light of his death. Barrett (1974) suggests that Paul's death may have reflected some discredit on the church, but even if his thesis is untenable in all its details, the epistle may still be seen as a restatement of Pauline theology following the destruction of Jerusalem.

In the light of the epistle's pseudonymity, this *Reading* has suggested that a historical reconstruction needs to be held together with a literary approach to the text. It has highlighted the liturgical context, both of the origin and of the continued significance of the epistle. It has suggested that the epistle is a text from a disciple of Paul who has seen the apostle's memory vindicated by the sacking of Jerusalem. It has suggested that the 'summing up of all things in Christ' is the theme of the epistle which is worked out in the Thanksgiving. Upon the basis of this the first readers – Jew and Gentile – were urged to lead a life worthy of those who, by the grace of God, were privileged to participate in God's 'summing up' of all things in Christ. We shall conclude this *Reading* with a few questions which take the literary and textual discussion a little further.

THE ABSENT AUTHOR

The epistle is not from the hand of Paul himself, and the deliberate ambiguity and pleonasm which characterize this piece of liturgical writing raise the issue of the nature of pseudepigraphical religious writing. The text does not simply recall historical events, but celebrates in the community's worship the story of God's action; this 'story' functions within worship, and does not simply repeat history '*wie es eigentlich gewesen ist*', 'as it really happened'. The epistle is a 'liturgical letter', and the early church's reluctance to put 'pen to paper' reflects a concern for immediacy which is rooted in the immediacy of the gospel itself. The written letter represented the presence of the absent author, and to read a letter during the worship of the church was to bring this directness into the immediate consciousness of the community; paradoxically, however, it also served to distance the possibility of immediacy. The question of Paul's status behind, around or within the text does arise, however. If the letter represented the author who was absent, does it, if it is pseudonymous, represent an author who is doubly absent, and does this diminish or enhance that person's authority? And, given the significance of *writing* in modern literary theory (see especially Derrida 1974, 1978), is not the concept of 'immediacy' compromised by the necessity of this 'originary supplement' (Derrida 1974: 313)?

THE LITURGICAL PURPOSE

The concept of 'story' brings together for the modern reader and scholar the approaches of historical criticism, literary appreciation and liturgical function of the text. 'Epistle', regarded in this thesis as 'liturgical letter', thus relates both to the genre of the letter in hellenistic culture and to liturgical practice. By it the community is enabled to function with a sense of God, and in a way which takes seriously life in the world. A further literary feature is also present in the text in the fact of the rhetorical context of 'summing up'. Kinneavy (1987) points to the relationship between 'faith' and 'persuasion', noting that the two words are related etymologically; he analyses many passages in the New Testament in which the persuasive element of Christian proclamation is to the fore. The liturgical context of the phrase 'to sum up all things in Christ' – within the Benediction at the start of Ephesians – keeps alive the purpose of the letter in its desire to persuade its readers of its truth and of the validity of its moral requirements. How do worship and rhetoric interact for modern readers?

'SUMMING UP' – THE WORD STUDY

The analysis of the verb 'to sum up' in 1.10 yielded a variety of possible meanings, all of which would be appropriate in the immediate context. The first is what might be called an *eschatological* meaning to be found in the two senses, 'sum up' and 'bring to a conclusion', in a rhetorical context; and also by that of 'crown'. The second area of theological interest is *creational.* It is related to the eschatological, in that it reflects an emphasis which is present in much eschatological thinking of the first century AD. It is present in the sense of 're-enact', or 'repeat', along with the sense of 'starting again'. This was derived largely from the analysis of the 'head' language in the Pauline corpus, in which it was shown that, by its association with 'beginning' in the Septuagint, it may bear the meaning of 'head' in the sense of 'source' or 'origin'. Here, the idea is that the time of the end repeats the time of creation; 'Endzeit wird Urzeit', as the Germans say. The third area is what might be termed *soteriological,* and this embraces the idea of 'uniting'. This is present also in rhetorical contexts in Greek literature, and it is worked out in Ephesians in the treatment of the relationship between Israel and the Gentiles, as well as in the ethical material. The sense of 'rule' may also be included here in that it is Christ's authority over the powers which makes possible the salvation he brings.

A further question is raised here, however, as a result of the observation by Handelman that 'the tendency to *gather* things *into a one* is . . . characteristic of Greek though in general: its movement towards the universal, the general, the univocal. The Rabbinic tendency, by contrast, is towards differentiation, metaphorical multiplicity, multiple meaning' (Handelman 1982: 33). 'Gathering into a one' is, of course, the same as 'summing up', however, and this rhetorical term has come to have christological significance in a text which attempts to show the unity of Jew and Gentile. If Handelman's understanding of Rabbinic Judaism is correct in this respect, then a 'Messiah' who achieves what God's chosen people precisely do not want, or who offers a kind of salvation which is fundamentally unappealing to the Jewish temperament, is hardly likely to find many followers. Could it be, though, that there is scope in Christian theology for a christology of difference and of diversity? That could be of great value in dialogue between ethnic groups, cultures and religions.

THE CONTENT OF THE THANKSGIVING

The 'summing up' of all things is said in Ephesians 1.10 to be effected both in heaven and on earth. The nature of this 'summing up' is then elaborated in Ephesians 2 in the exposition of the Thanksgiving. The 'summing up' 'in heaven' is set out in the first ten verses as the raising to life and the setting in the heavenlies of the people of God. In this way humanity is reconciled with God. This necessarily involves a demonstration of power over death, and of authority over all spiritual forces, who also inhabit the heavenly realm.

The 'summing up' *on earth* is the reconciliation between the two races, Jew and Gentile. In the background of the writer's understanding of the Pauline gospel of human reconciliation is the breaking down of the dividing wall which separates Jews from Gentiles. Of the various possibilities for interpreting this image, the most likely is the 'fence' which divided the Court of Israel from the Court of the Gentiles in the Temple at Jerusalem.

Earthly reconciliation here is on the basis of the reconciliation which has already been brought about between humanity and God, for the starting point in the text is the body of Christ which was both sacrificed and raised. Upon this basis is the appeal made to both Jewish and Gentile Christians to recognize their common experience of initiation into the death and resurrection of Christ. If both can share that experience, then both must be one. The body which is thus at one with itself and reconciled to God is therefore one building at the hands of Christ; indeed, it is one Temple; moreover, it exhibits an organic kind of growth as a body.

This is a suggestive set of metaphors for the unity of the human race. Contemporary readers may wish to note Said's reference (1993: 368) to Hayden White's observation that 'all historical writing *is* writing and delivers figural language and representational tropes'. Is it possible for Christians to tell the story of God in such a way that the reality thus created does not further exclude those throughout the whole world and in every continent who are already aliens in their own country and culture? How seriously is the new community of the 'perfect human' prepared to take this language of the oneness of the human race, given its ethnic diversity and a context of increasing tension?

THE ETHICS OF EPHESIANS

We noted earlier (in chapter 5) that the text of Ephesians does not know of any distinction between 'fact' and 'value', and such a distinction is becoming increasingly difficult in the light of our awareness of the imperialistic claims of Western culture, as chronicled by Said (1978, 1993) among others. The ethical material in Ephesians is introduced by an exhortation to 'walk worthy of the calling with which you are called'. The text then develops an understanding of the 'summing up' which entails the church's participation in that divine plan by living an appropriate lifestyle. The church is to be the 'perfect man' of Ephesians 4.13, so the lists of vices and virtues are to be seen as forwarding this purpose.

It is in the household code, however, that the readers are especially urged to live a life which demonstrates a moral participation in the divine plan. The code from the Epistle to the Colossians is deliberately adapted to urge mutual submission; the readers are to emulate Christ in their own behaviour and so 'grow up' into him. The marriage imagery, in particular, indicates how believers are to submit themselves to each other, rather than simply follow conventional patterns of 'hierarchical' submission. This way of life gives expression to the sacrificial, submissive love which was shown by Christ in the love which brought the church into being.

It cannot be said that Ephesians is either a feminist or a politically radical document; the only sexual relationship that is dealt with in it is marriage. Nevertheless, the impetus to revise an earlier text in the direction of a greater inclusiveness is here. Can this speak promisingly to those who must take on into hitherto unmapped territory the quest for a new sexual and ethnic morality which will meet the needs of an age which in some respects is very different from, and in others very similar to, the one for which Ephesians was written?

THE ARMOUR OF GOD

The corporate image of the armour of God draws together the eschatological, creational and soteriological understandings of the 'summing up', as well as its ethical implications. The soldier in God's complete armour is clad, not in individual virtues, but in those characteristics of the gospel which are distinctive of the whole community. The separate items of the armour – truth, righteousness, the gospel of peace, faith, salvation and the Spirit's sword – are attributes and characteristics of God, which God shares first with Christ, and then with those who by baptism are incorporate in Christ. The image may be masculine, strong and powerful, but the soldier in complete armour is the destiny of the church's growth, the 'perfect man' of Ephesians 4.13, the new Adam and Eve, the Messiah who brings salvation for all, and who incorporates all. The question for today is, in what ways can this image – and this whole letter – still function for Christian worship as an image of persuasive power for the unity of the whole of humankind?

Bibliography

Abbott, T.K. (1897) *The Epistles to the Ephesians and Colossians*, The International Critical Commentary, Edinburgh: T. & T. Clark.

Anderson, A.A. (1972) *The Book of Psalms*, New Century Bible, London: Oliphants.

Arndt, W.F. and Gingrich, F.W. (1957) *A Greek–English Lexicon of the New Testament*, Chicago: University of Chicago Press.

Arnold, C.E. (1987) 'The "Exorcism" of Ephesians 6.12 in Recent Research', *Journal for the Study of the New Testament* 30.

Asting, R. (1930) *Die Heiligkeit im Urchristentum*, FRLANT 45, Göttingen: Vandenhoeck & Ruprecht.

Auerbach, E. (1968) *Mimesis*, Princeton: Princeton University Press.

Aulén, G. (1975) *Christus Victor*, London: SPCK.

Bailey, J.L. and Vander Broek, L.D. (1992) *Literary Forms in the New Testament*, London: SPCK.

Barr, J. (1961) *The Semantics of Biblical Language*, Oxford: Oxford University Press.

—— (1973) *The Bible and the Modern World*, London: SCM Press.

Barrett, C.K. (1962) *From First Adam to Last*, London: A. & C. Black.

—— (1974) 'Pauline Controversies in the Post-Pauline Period', *New Testament Studies* 20.

Barth, K. (1960) *Church Dogmatics III.2*, Edinburgh: T. & T. Clark.

Barth, M. (1960) *The Broken Wall, a Study of the Epistle to the Ephesians*, London: Collins.

—— (1974) *Ephesians*, The Anchor Bible, New York: Doubleday & Co.

—— (1985) 'Traditions in Ephesians', *New Testament Studies* 30.

Baur, F.C. (1845) *Paulus der Apostel Jesu Christi*, Stuttgart: Becker & Muller.

Beardslee, W.A. (1970) *Literary Criticism of the New Testament*, Philadelphia: Fortress Press.

Bedale, S. (1954) 'The Meaning of Kephale in the Pauline Epistles', *Journal of Theological Studies* (new series) 5.

Best, E. (1972) *The First and Second Epistles to the Thessalonians*, London: A. & C. Black.

Blass, F., Debrunner, A. and Funk, R.W. (1961) *A Greek Grammar of the New Testament and other Early Christian Literature*, Chicago: University of Chicago Press.

Bonhöffer, A. (1911) *Epiktet und das neue Testament, religionsgeschichtliche Versuche und Vorarbeiten X*, Giessen: Töpelmann.

Bornkamm, G. (1948) 'Die Häresie der Kolosser', *Theologische Literaturzeiting* 73.

Bousset, W. (1901) 'Die Himmelsreise der Seele', *Archiv für Religionswissenschaft* 4.

Bowker, J. (1978) *The Religious Imagination and the Sense of God*, Oxford: Oxford University Press.

Brox, N. (1975) *Falsche Vervasserangaben*, Stuttgart: Stuttgarter Bibelstudien 79.

Bultmann, R. (1910) *Der Stil der paulinischen Predigt und das kynisch–stoisch Diatribe*, Göttingen: Vandenhoeck & Ruprecht.

——— (1924) 'Das Problem der Ethik bei Paulus', *Zeitschrift für die neutestamentliche Wissenschaft* 23.

——— (1952) *Theology of the New Testament*, London: SCM Press.

Burkert, W. (1961) 'Hellenistische Pseudopythagorica', *Philologus* 105.

Cadbury, H.J. (1959) 'The Dilemma of Ephesians', *New Testament Studies* 5.

Caird, G.B. (1964) 'The Descent of Christ in Eph 4.7–11', *Studia Evangelica* 2.

——— (1976) *Paul's Letters from Prison*, New Clarendon Bible Series, Oxford: Oxford University Press.

Campenhausen, H. von (1969) *Ecclesiastical Authority and Spiritual Power*, London: A. & C. Black.

Carr, A.W. (1981) *Angels and Principalities*, SNTS Monograph Series 42, Cambridge: Cambridge University Press.

Carrington, P. (1940) *The Primitive Christian Catechism*, Cambridge: Cambridge University Press.

Chadwick, H. (1960) 'Die Absicht des Epheserbriefes', *Zeitschrift für die neutestamentliche Wissenschaft* 51.

Coleridge, H.N. (ed.) (1835) *Specimens of the Table Talk of the Late Samuel Taylor Coleridge*, London: Humphrey Milford, and Oxford: Oxford University Press.

Conzelmann, H. (1962) *Der Epheserbrief*, Neues Testament Deutsch 8, 9th edition, Göttingen: Vandenhoeck & Ruprecht.

Coutts, J. (1956–7) 'Ephesians 1.3–14 and I Peter 1.3–12', *New Testament Studies* 9.

——— (1957–8) 'The Relationship of Ephesians and Colossians', *New Testament Studies* 4.

Cross F.L. (ed.) (1956) *Studies in Ephesians*, London: A.R. Mowbray & Sons.

Dahl, N.A. (1951) 'Adresse und Proömium des Epheserbriefes, *Theologische Zeitschrift* 7.

Davies, W.D. (1970) *Paul and Rabbinic Judaism*, 3rd edition, London: SPCK.

Derrida, J. (1974) *Of Grammatology*, Baltimore: Johns Hopkins University Press.

——— (1978) *Writing and Difference*, London: Routledge & Kegan Paul.

Dibelius, M. (1935) *From Tradition to Gospel*, London: Scribner & Sons.

Dibelius, M. and Greeven, H., (1953) *An die Kolosser, Epheser, an Philemon*, Handbuch zum Neuen Testament, 3rd edition, Tübingen: J.C.B. Mohr (Paul Siebeck).

Diels, H., ed. Kranz, W. (1934–54) *Fragmente der Vorsokratiker,* Berlin: Weidmann.

Dinkler, E. (1952) 'Zum Problem der Ethick bei Paulus: Rechtsnahme und Rechtsverzicht (I Cor 6.1–11),' *Zeitschrift für Theologie und Kirche.*

Doležel, L. and Bailey, R.W. (1969) *Statistics and Style,* New York: American Elsevier Publishing Co.

Doty, W.G. (1973) *Letters in Primitive Christianity,* Philadelphia: Fortress Press.

Drewery, B. (1988) 'Arnold Toynbee and the Philosphy of History', *Modern Churchman* (new series) 30/1.

Dunn, J.D.G. (1977) *Unity and Diversity in the New Testament,* London: SCM Press.

Eagleton, T. (1983) *Literary Theory, an Introduction,* Oxford: Basil Blackwell & Sons.

Easton, B.S. (1932) 'The New Testament Ethical Lists', *Journal of Biblical Literature* 51.

Edwards, David L. (1992) *The Real Jesus,* London: Fount.

Erasmus, D. (1519, repr. 1540) *In Novum Testamentum Adnotationes,* Basel: Froben.

Ernesti, H.F.T.L. (1880) *Die Ethik des Apostels Paulus in ihren Grundzügen dargestellt,* 3rd edition, Göttingen.

Ernst, J. (1970) *Pleroma und Pleroma Christi,* Regensburg: Regensburger Bibelstudien.

Evans, C.F. (1971) *Is 'Holy Scripture' Christian?,* London: SCM Press.

—— (1975) 'Hermeneutics', *Epworth Review,* 2/1 (repr. in Evans, C.F. (1977) *Explorations in Theology* 2, London: SCM Press.)

Evanson, E. (1792) *The Dissonance of the Four Generally Received Evangelists and the Evidence of their Respective Authority Examined,* Ipswich.

Ewald, P. (1910) *Die Briefe des Paulus an die Epheser, Kolosser und Philemon,* 2nd edition, ed. Zahn, T., Leipzig: Deichert.

Fischer, K.M. (1973) *Tendenz und Absicht des Epheserbriefes,* Forschungen zur Religion und Literatur des Alten und Neuen Testaments 111, Göttingen: Vandenhoeck & Ruprecht.

Fowler, A. (1982) *Kinds of Literature,* Oxford: Clarendon Press.

Frye, N., Baker, S. and Perkins, G. (eds) (1985), *The Harper Handbook to Literature,* New York: Harper & Row.

Funk, R.W. (1966) *Language, Hermeneutic and Word of God,* New York: Harper & Row.

Furnish, V.P. (1968) *Theology and Ethics in Paul,* Nashville: Abingdon Press.

Gadamer, H.-G. (1975) *Truth and Method,* New York: Seabury Press.

Gardner, H. (1982) *In Defence of the Imagination,* Clarendon Press, Oxford: 1982.

Gnilka, J. (1971) *Der Epheserbrief,* Freiburg: Herders Theologische Kommentar zum Neuen Testament.

Goodspeed, E.J. (1933) *The Meaning of Ephesians,* Chicago: Chicago University Press.

—— (1956) *The Key to Ephesians,* Chicago: Chicago University Press.

Grundmann, W. (1959) 'Die *NHΠIOI* in der urchristlichen Paranese', *New Testament Studies* 5.

Gudemann, A. (1894) *Literary Frauds among the Greeks: Classical Studies in Honour of H. Drisler*, New York.

Guiver, G. (1993) 'Daily Prayer: A Brief History', in Roberts, P., Stancliffe, D. and Stevenson, K. (eds) *Something Understood*, London: Hodder & Stoughton.

Guthrie, D. (1964) *New Testament Introduction*, London: Inter Varsity Press.

Güttgemanns, E. (1971) *Offene Fragen zur Formgeschichte des Evangeliums*, 2nd edition, Munich: Kaiser Verlag.

Hammond, G. (1983) 'The Bible and Literary Criticism', *Critical Quarterly*, 25/2–3.

Handelman, S. (1982) *The Slayers of Moses*, Albany: State University of New York Press.

Hanson, S. (1946) *The Unity of the Church in the New Testament*, Uppsala and Copenhagen: Almqvist.

Harnack, A. (1910) *Das Problem des zweiten Thessalonikerbriefs*, Berlin: Sitzungsberichte der Akademie der Wissenschaften.

Hengel, M. (1978) 'Hymn and Christology', *Studia Biblica* III.19.

Hirsch, E.D. (1967) *Validity in Interpretation*, New Haven: Yale University Press.

Holtzmann, H.J. (1872) *Kritik der Epheser- und Kolosserbriefe*, Leipzig: Engelman.

Houlden, J.L. (1977) *Paul's Letters from Prison*, Pelican New Testament Commentaries, London: SCM Press.

Howard, G. (1974) 'The Head/Body Metaphor of Ephesians', *New Testament Studies* 20.

Hunter, A.M. (1961) *Paul and his Predecessors*, London: SCM Press.

Jacoby, F. (1923–) *Die Fragmente der griechischen Historiker*, Berlin and Leiden: E.J. Brill.

Jaeger, W. (1953) *Die Theologie der frühen griechischen Denker*, Stuttgart.

Jahrbuch für Antike und Christentum 8/9 (1965–6).

Jeremias, J. (1958) 'Chiasmus in den Paulusbriefen', *Zeitschrift für die neutestamentliche Wissenschaft* 49.

Jervell, J. (1960) *Imago Dei*, Göttingen: Vandenhoeck & Ruprecht.

Jones, C., Wainwright, G. and Yarnold, E.J. (eds) (1978) *The Study of Liturgy*, London: SPCK.

Jülicher, A. (1904) *Introduction to the New Testament*, London: J.C.B Mohr.

Kamlah, E. (1964) *Die Form der katalogischen Paranese im Neuen Testament*, Wissenschaftliche Untersuchungen zum Neuen Testament 7, Tübingen: J.C.B. Mohr (Paul Siebeck).

Käsemann, E. (1932) *Leib und Leib Christi*, Tübingen: J.C.B. Mohr (Paul Siebeck).

—— (1949) 'Ernst Percy: Die Probleme der Kolosser- und Epheserbriefe', *Gnomon* 21.

—— (1958) 'Epheserbrief', *Religion in Geschichte und Gegenwart* 2.

—— (1961) 'Das Interpretationsproblem des Epheserbriefes', *Theologische Literaturzeitung* 86.

—— (1980) *Commentary on Romans*, London: SCM Press.

Kaufmann, G. (1971) 'What Shall We Do With the Bible?', *Interpretation* 25/1.

Kavanagh, A. (1984) *On Liturgical Theology*, New York: Pueblo Publishing Co.

Kennedy, G.A. (1984) *New Testament Interpretation through Rhetorical Criticism*, Chapel Hill and London: University of North Carolina Press.

Kinneavy, J.L. (1987) *Greek Rhetorical Origins of Christian Faith, an Enquiry*, New York and Oxford: Oxford University Press.

Kirby, J.C. (1968) *Ephesians, Baptism and Pentecost*, London: SPCK.

Kittel, G. and Friedrich, G.(1964–74) *Theological Dictionary of the New Testament* (= TDNT), Grand Rapids: Eerdmans.

Knitter, P.F. (1985) *No Other Name*, London: SCM Press.

Knox, J. (1935, 2nd edn 1959) *Philemon among the Letters of Paul*, New York and Nashville: Abingdon Press.

—— (1942) *Marcion and the New Testament*, Chicago: Chicago University Press.

Krentz, E. (1975) *The Historical-Critical Method*, Philadelphia: Fortress Press.

Kümmel, W.G. (1975) *Introduction to the New Testament*, London: SCM Press.

Lake, K. (1976) *The Apostolic Fathers*, Loeb Classical Library, Cambridge, MA and London: Harvard University Press and William Heineman Ltd.

Lampe, G.W.H. (1967) *The Seal of the Spirit*, 2nd edition, London: SPCK.

Lawson, J. (1948) *The Biblical Theology of Irenaeus*, London: Epworth Press.

Lessing, G.E. (1774–8) *Fragmente eines Unbekannten*, Wolfenbüttel.

Liddell, H.G. and Scott, R. (1864) *A Greek–English Lexicon*, Oxford: Oxford University Press.

Lietzmann, H. (1933) *An die Römer*, 4th edition, Handbuch zum Neuen Testament 8, Tübingen: J.C.B. Mohr (Paul Siebeck).

Lincoln, A.T. (1981) *Paradise Now and Not Yet*, SNTS Monograph Series 43, Cambridge: Cambridge University Press.

Lindars, B. (1961) *New Testament Apologetic*, London: SCM Press.

Lindemann, A. (1975) *Die Aufhebung der Zeit*, Gutersloh: Gerd Mohn.

Lohmeyer, E. (1926) 'Das Proömium des Epheserbriefes', *Theologische Blätter* 5.

Lohse, E. (1971) *Colossians and Philemon*, Philadelphia: Fortress Press.

Malina, B.J. (1983) *The New Testament World: Insights from Cultural Anthropology*, London: SCM Press.

Marshall, I.H. (ed.) (1977) *New Testament Interpretation*, Exeter: Paternoster Press.

Martin, R.P. (1968) 'An Epistle in Search of a Life Setting', *Expository Times* 79.

Masson, C. (1953) *L'Épitre de Saint Paul aux Éphesiens*, Commentaire du Nouveau Testament 9, Neuchâtel: Delachaux et Niestlé.

—— (1957) *I & II Thessaloniens*, Commentaire du Nouveau Testament 11a, Neuchâtel and Paris: Delachaux & Niestlé.

Maurer, C. (1951–2) 'Der Hymnus von Eph 1 als Schlüssel zum ganzen Brief', *Evangelische Theologie* 11.

McKelvey, R.J. (1969) *The New Temple*, Oxford: Oxford University Press.

Merklein, H. (1973) *Christus und die Kirche: die theologische Grundstruktur des Epheserbriefes, nach Epheserbrief 2.11–18*, Stuttgart: Stuttgarter Bibelstudien 66.

Metzger, B.M. (1971) *A Textual Commentary on the Greek New Testament*, New York and London: United Bible Societies.

—— (1980) *Lexical Aids for Students of NT Greek*, Oxford: Basil Blackwell.

Meyer, R.P. (1977) *Kirche und Mission im Epheserbrief*, Stuttgart: Stuttgarter Bibelstudien 86.

Migne, J.P. (1844–64) *Patrologia Graeca* (= PG), Paris: Garnier Fratres.

—— (1857–66) *Patrologia Latina* (= PL), Paris: Garnier Fratres.

Minear, P.S. (1971) *The Obedience of Faith*, Studies in Biblical Theology, 2nd series, 19, London: SCM Press.

Mitton, C.L. (1951) *The Epistle to the Ephesians: Its Authorship, Origin and Purpose*, Oxford: Oxford University Press.

—— (1976) *Ephesians*, New Century Bible, London: Oliphants.

Moore, S.D. (1992) *Mark and Luke in Poststructuralist Perspectives*, New Haven and London: Yale University Press.

Morgan, R. and Barton, J. (1988) *Biblical Interpretation*, The Oxford Bible Series, Oxford: Oxford University Press.

Moran, G. (1992) *Uniqueness*, New York: Orbis Books.

Moule, C.F.D. (1962) *The Birth of the New Testament*, London: A. & C. Black.

—— (1977) *The Origin of Christology*, Cambridge: Cambridge University Press.

Moulton, W.F. and Geden, A.S. (1963) *A Concordance to the Greek New Testament*, 4th edition, Edinburgh: T. & T. Clark.

Mussner, F. (1955) *Christus, das All und die Kirche: Studien zur Theologie des Epheserbriefes*, Trier: Trierer Theologische Studien 5.

Neill, S. (1966) *The Interpretation of the New Testament 1861–1961*, Oxford: Oxford University Press.

Nineham, D.E. (1956) 'The Case Against Pauline Authorship', in Cross, F.L. (ed.) *Studies in Ephesians*, London: A.R. Mowbray & Co. Ltd.

—— (1978) *The Use and Abuse of the Bible*, London: SPCK.

Otto, R. (1923) *The Idea of the Holy*, London: Oxford University Press.

Pagels, E.H. (1975) *The Gnostic Paul: Gnostic Exegesis of the Pauline Letters*, Philadelphia: Fortress Press.

Patte, D. (1976) *What Is Structural Exegesis?*, Philadelphia: Fortress Press.

Pauly, A. (rev. Wissowa, G. von) (1903–70) *Realenzyklopädie der klassischen Altertumswissenschaft*, Stuttgart: Metzler.

Peake, A.S. (1917–18), 'The Quintessence of Paulinism', *Bulletin of the John Rylands Library* 4.

Percy, E. (1946) *Die Probleme der Kolosser- und Epheserbriefe*, Lund: Skrifter utgivna av Kungl. Humanistika Vetensskapssamfundet XXXIX.

Perrin, N. (1970) *What Is Redaction Criticism?*, London: SPCK.

Peterson, N.R. (1978) *Literary Criticism for New Testament Critics*, Philadelphia: Fortress Press.

Pokorny, P. (1964) *Der Epheserbrief und die Gnosis*, Berlin: Evangelische Verlagsanstalt.

Powis Smith, J.M. (1928–9) 'The Chosen People', *American Journal of Semitic Languages* 45.

Preisker, H. (1949) *Das Ethos des Urchristentums*, 2nd edition, Gutersloh: Bertelsmann.

Ramsey, A.M. (1936) *The Gospel and the Catholic Church*, London: Longmans, Green & Co.

Ranke, L. von (1874) *Geschichten der romanischen und germanischen Volker*, Leipzig.

Reed, B.D. (1978) *The Dynamics of Religion*, London: Darton, Longman & Todd.

Reitzenstein, R. (1927) *Hellenistische Mysterien-religionen*, Leipzig: Teubner.

Robinson, J.A. (1904) *St Paul's Epistle to the Ephesians*, 2nd edition, London: Macmillan.

Robinson, J.A.T. (1952) *The Body*, London: SCM Press.

—— (1976) *Redating the New Testament*, London: SCM Press.

Robinson, J.M. (ed.) (1977) *The Nag Hammadi Library*, London: E.J. Brill.

Rohde, J. (1968) *Rediscovering the Teaching of the Evangelists*, London: SCM Press.

Roon, A. van (1974) *The Authenticity of Ephesians*, Supplements to Novum Testamentum 39, Leiden: E.J. Brill.

Rowley, H.H. (1950) *The Biblical Doctrine of Election*, London: Lutterworth Press.

Rückert, L.J. von (1834) *Der Brief Pauli an die Epheser*.

Russell, D.S. (1971) *The Method and Message of Jewish Apocalyptic*, London: SCM Press.

Said, E.W. (1978) *Orientalism*, London: Routledge & Kegan Paul.

—— (1993) *Culture and Imperialism*, London: Chatto & Windus.

Sampley, J.P. (1971) *And the Two Shall Become One Flesh*, SNTS Monograph Series 16, Cambridge: Cambridge University Press.

Sanday W. and Headlam, A.C. (1914) *A Critical and Exegetical Commentary on the Epistle to the Romans*, Edinburgh: T. & T. Clark.

Schama, S. (1991) *Dead Certainties, or Unwarranted Speculations*, London: Granta Books.

Schille, G. (1953) *Liturgisches Gut im Epheserbrief*, unpublished dissertation, Göttingen.

—— (1957) 'Der Autor des Epheserbriefes', *Theologische Literaturzeitung* 82.

—— (1965) *Frühchristliche Hymnen*, Berlin: Evangelische Verlagsanstalt.

Schlier, H. (1930) *Christus und die Kirche im Epheserbrief*, Beitrage zur historischen Theologie 6, Tübingen: J.C.B. Mohr.

—— (1963) *Der Brief an die Epheser*, 4th edition, Düsseldorf: Patmos Verlag.

Schnackenburg, R. (1982) *Der Brief an die Epheser*, Evangelisch-katholisches Kommentar zum neuen Testament, Neukirchen, Zürich, Köln: Benzinger Verlag.

Schubert, P.S. (1939) *The Form and Function of the Pauline Thanksgiving*, ZNW Beiheft 20, Berlin: Töpelmann.

Schwegler, F.K.A. (1846) *Das Nachapostolischer Zeitalter*, Tübingen: Ludwig Friedrich Fues.

Schweitzer, A. (1910, 3rd edition 1954) *The Quest of the Historical Jesus*, London: A. & C. Black.

—— (1931, 2nd edition 1953) *The Mysticism of Paul the Apostle*, London: A. & C. Black.

Selwyn, E.G. (1947) *The First Epistle of Peter*, 2nd edition, London: Macmillan.

Speyer, W. (1971) *Die literarische Fälschung im heidnischen und christlichen Altertum*, Munich: Beck.

Steiner, G. (1989) *Real Presences*, London: Faber & Faber.

—— (1993) *After Babel*, 2nd edition, London and New York: Oxford University Press.

Stevenson, K.W. (1982) *Nuptial Blessing*, Alcuin Club Collections 64, London: SPCK.

Strack, H.L. and Billerbeck, P. (1922–61) *Kommentar zum neuen Testament aus Talmud und Midrasch*, Munich: Beck.

Strauss, D.F., trans. Eliot, G. (1846) *The Life of Jesus Critically Examined*, London: Chapman Brothers.

Stroup, G.W. (1975) 'A Bibliographical Critique', *Theology Today* 32.

—— (1981) *The Promise of Narrative Theology*, London: SCM Press.

Swete, H.B. (ed.) (1880) *Theodore of Mopsuestia, In Epistolas 13 Pauli Commentarii*, Cambridge: Cambridge University Press.

Synge, F.C. (1954) *St Paul's Epistle to the Ephesians*, London: SPCK.

Taylor, M.C. (1984) *Erring: a Postmodern A/theology*, Chicago and London: University of Chicago Press.

Thiering, B. (1993) *Jesus, the Man*, London: Corgi Books.

Thrower, J. (1971) *A Short History of Western Atheism*, The Humanist Library, London: Pemberton Books.

Toynbee, A.J. (1934–61) *A Study of History*, Oxford: Oxford University Press.

Trench, R.C. (1860) *Synonyms of the New Testament*, Cambridge: Macmillan.

Ussher, J. (1650–4) *Annales Veteris et Novi Testamenti*, London: Crook.

Vermes, G. (1962) *The Dead Sea Scrolls in English*, Harmondsworth: Penguin Books.

Via, D.O. (1967) *The Parables*, Philadelphia: Fortress Press.

—— (1975) *Kerygma and Comedy in the New Testament*, Philadelphia: Fortress Press.

Vögtle, A. (1936) *Die Tugend- und Lasterkataloge im neuen Testament exegetisch, religionsgeschichtlich und formgeschichtlich untersucht*, Münster: Aschendorff Neutestamentliche Abhandlungen 16:4–5.

Wainwright, G. (1980) *Doxology*, London: Epworth Press.

Weinreich, O. (1969) *Neue Urkunden zur Serapis-Religion*, Amsterdam: Ausgewählte Schriften I, 410.43.

Wette, W. de (1847) *Exegetisches Handbuch zum neuen Testament*, Leipzig: Weidmann.

White, J.L. (1972) *The Form and Function of the Body of the Greek Letter*, Montana: Scholars Press.

Wibbing, S. (1959) *Die Tugend- und Lasterkataloge im neuen Testament*, Beihefte zur Zeitschrift für die NT Wissenschaft 25, Berlin: Töpelmann.

Wilder, A.N. (1964) *Early Christian Rhetoric*, London: SCM Press.

Wiles, M. (1967) *The Divine Apostle*, Cambridge: Cambridge University Press.

Williams, R.D. (1979) *The Wound of Knowledge*, London: Darton, Longman & Todd.

Wilson, A.N. (1992) *Jesus*, London: Sinclair Stevenson.

Wink, W. (1975) *The Bible in Human Transformation*, Philadelphia: Fortress Press.

Wright, N.T. (1992) *Who Was Jesus?*, London: SPCK.

Young, F.M. (1982) *Can These Dry Bones Live?*, London: SCM Press.

Zerwick, M. and Grosvenor, M. (1980) *An Analysis of the Greek New Testament*, Rome: Biblical Institute Press.

Ziesler, J.A. (1972) *The Meaning of Righteousness in Paul*, SNTS Monograph Series 20, Cambridge: Cambridge University Press.

Index